D1009019

LAS VEGAS

ENCOUNTER

SARA BENSON

Las Vegas Encounter

Published by Lonely Planet Publications Pty Ltd
ABN 36 005 607 983

Australia	Head Office, Locked Bag 1, Footscray, Vic 3011
	☎ 03 8379 8000 fax 03 8379 8111
	talk2us@lonelyplanet.com.au
USA	150 Linden St, Oakland, CA 94607
	☎ 510 250 6400
	toll free 800 275 8555
	fax 510 893 8572
	info@lonelyplanet.com
UK	2nd fl, 186 City Rd
	London EC1V 2NT
	☎ 020 7106 2100 fax 020 7106 2101
	go@lonelyplanet.co.uk

This title was commissioned in Lonely Planet's Oakland office and produced by: **Commissioning Editor** Suki Gear **Coordinating Editors** Susie Ashworth, Carolyn Boicos **Coordinating Cartographer** Andy Rojas **Assisting Cartographer** Jolyon Philcox **Layout Designer** Pablo Gastar **Senior Editors** Helen Christinis, Katie Lynch **Managing Cartographer** Alison Lyall **Cover Designer** Pepi Bluck **Project Managers** Eoin Dunlevy, Fabrice Rocher **Managing Layout Designers** Laura Jane, Celia Wood

Thanks to Alex Acuna, Tamar Aprahamian, Christi Braginton, Andrea Dutcher, Ashley Farkas, Jessica Gildar, Matthew Griffin, Lisa Knights, Charity Mackinnon, Mike McKiski, Michelle Mosbacher, Wayne Murphy, Jennifer Polito, Martine Power, Raphael Richards, Rosalind Terlitzky

ISBN 978-1-74104-993-0

Printed by Hang Tai Printing Company, China.

HOW TO USE THIS BOOK

Color-Coding & Maps
Color-coding is used for symbols on maps and in the text that they relate to (eg all eating venues on the maps and in the text are given a green knife and fork symbol).

Prices
Multiple prices listed with reviews (eg $10/5 or $10/5/20) indicate adult/child, adult/concession or adult/child/family.

Send us your feedback We love to hear from readers — your comments help make our books better. We read every word you send us, and we always guarantee that your feedback goes straight to the appropriate authors. The most useful submissions are rewarded with a free book. To send us your updates and find out about Lonely Planet events, newsletters and travel news visit our award-winning website: *lonelyplanet.com/contact*.

Note: We may edit, reproduce and incorporate your comments in Lonely Planet products such as guidebooks, websites and digital products, so let us know if you don't want your comments reproduced or your name acknowledged. For a copy of our privacy policy visit *lonelyplanet.com/privacy*.

SARA BENSON

First awestruck by the neon lights of the Strip
during a cross-country trek from Chicago to
California, Sara had a serendipitous one-night
stand with Sin City that soon became a torrid love
affair. Now she travels down to the desert every
chance she gets, and has racked up more hours
gambling, carousing and wandering around Las
Vegas than she'll ever admit to her grandmother.
She and her entourage have spent many a lost
weekend nightclub-hopping down the Strip,
feasting at star chefs' tables and playing poker
until the wee hours in downtown's Glitter Gulch.

Sara is also an avid outdoor enthusiast. Her articles have featured on
popular travel websites and in magazines and newspapers from coast
to coast, including the *Las Vegas Review-Journal*, *Los Angeles Times* and
National Geographic Traveler. The author of more than 30 travel and non-
fiction books, Sara also wrote Lonely Planet's *Las Vegas City Guide*.

SARA'S THANKS

Many thanks to all of the Las Vegas residents who helped my research,
especially those who took time out to be interviewed and photographed
for this book. Without Mike Connolly, Anna Muir and Suki Gear, creating
this book just wouldn't have been so much fun.

THE PHOTOGRAPHER

Jerry Alexander makes his home in the Napa Valley, California. He and
his wife, Thanaphon, have just completed building a home in Chiang
Mai, Thailand. Jerry grows grapes in the Napa Valley and after harvest he
and his wife head back to Thailand to see family and friends – and make
images around Southeast Asia. Jerry has worked on six individual titles
for Lonely Planet and contributed to many of Lonely Planet's guidebooks
as well.

Cover photograph Craps table, Andrew Manley/iStockPhoto. **Internal photographs** p3, p41, p75, p124, p141 Sara Benson;
p162 David Crotty; p22 Rouse Photography; p63 Wynn Las Vegas. All other photographs by Lonely Planet Images and Jerry
Alexander except p20 Jeff Greenberg; p14, p55, p60, p74, p151, p155, p159, p172 Ray Laskowitz; p19 Curtis Martin; p156
David Tomlinson

All images are copyright of the photographers unless otherwise indicated. Many of the images in this guide are available for
licensing from **Lonely Planet Images:** www.lonelyplanetimages.com.

Enjoy a slice of the Big Apple at New York–New York (p53)

CONTENTS

Why is our travel information the best in the world? It's simple: our authors are passionate, dedicated travelers. They don't take freebies in exchange for positive coverage so you can be sure the advice you're given is impartial. They travel widely to all the popular spots, and off the beaten track. They don't research using just the internet or phone. They discover new places not included in any other guidebook. They personally visit thousands of hotels, restaurants, palaces, trails, galleries, temples and more. They speak with dozens of locals every day to make sure you get the kind of insider knowledge only a local could tell you. They take pride in getting all the details right, and in telling it how it is. Think you can do it? Find out how at **lonelyplanet.com**.

THIS IS LAS VEGAS

A Bible-toting Elvis kisses a giddy couple who've just pledged eternity in the Chapel of Love. A blue-haired granny feeds nickels into a slot machine while chain-smoking and slugging gin-and-tonics. A porn star saunters by a nightclub's velvet rope. Blink, and you'll miss it. Sleep? Fuhgeddaboutit.

Vegas is the ultimate escape. A few frenzied sleepless nights here can be more intoxicating than a week-long bender elsewhere. Let the everyday rules of behavior slide a little, like a burlesque dancer's feather boa. Be as naughty as you wanna be, and make your most devilish fantasies come true. Sin City stands ready to give you an alibi: what happens here, stays here. Who can resist such seductive temptation?

The defining mood of Las Vegas is euphoria, from the 19th-century silver miners looking to strike the mother lode to the mobsters, movie stars, showgirls and crooners who lived it up here during the 'fabulous' 1950s heyday. Eccentric billionaire Howard Hughes helped the city clean up its act when he ushered in corporate ownership of casinos, and soon afterward middle America invaded the hoity-toity Strip in their polyester tracksuits with screaming rug rats in tow. As the 20th century raced toward its end, megaresorts on par with Macau and Monte Carlo began to spike the Strip's skyline. Every decade has made Las Vegas more of a boomtown than ever before.

This city demands a suspension of disbelief, so don't take it too seriously. In Sin City, fate is decided by the spin of a roulette wheel. It's a place where lucky schmucks are treated like royalty and the rich wager thousands on a single roll of the dice. But in the end, it doesn't matter if you play the penny slots or lay down a bankroll at the poker tables, it's a sure thing you'll still leave town believing you've just had the most frenzied, fast-paced and fantastical time of your life.

Top left Indulge your inner vamp at Pussycat Dolls Lounge (p153) **Bottom left** Savor the spectacle of Las Vegas

LAS VEGAS LAYOUT

Sprawled immodestly along Las Vegas Blvd, the Strip is constantly re-inventing itself, becoming ever more spectacular – and more of a spectacle. Every casino hotel has its own attractions, with plenty of action besides gaming. The Strip runs south to Mandalay Bay and north to the Stratosphere. Its nerve center is the intersection with Flamingo Rd.

Downtown presides over the distant north end of the tourist corridor, with the canopied Fremont Street Experience streaking down the middle of Glitter Gulch. The city's historic quarter is preferred by serious gamblers, who find faux volcanoes beneath them; the smoky, low-ceilinged casinos have changed little over the years. East of Las Vegas Blvd, Fremont St is undergoing a renaissance of cool, with independent bars and nightclubs popping up.

The 18b Arts District, emerging around the intersection of Main St and Charleston Blvd, is ground zero for hipsters, artists and alt-cultural types. The desolate stretch of Las Vegas Blvd between downtown and the Strip is nicknamed the Naked City. These downtrodden blocks sport tattered cheap motels, tattoo parlors and drive-thru wedding chapels.

East of the Strip, the University of Nevada (UNLV) campus attracts youthful carpetbaggers along Maryland Parkway. Anchored by the Las Vegas Convention Center, Paradise Rd streams south past the Hard Rock casino hotel into the Fruit Loop, the epicenter of the LGBT community.

West of the Strip, the Palms and Rio casino hotels rule the roost; many of Sin City's strip clubs and sex shops are hidden in industrial backstreets and strip malls. Burgeoning suburbs include Henderson, southeast of McCarran International Airport, and moneyed Summerlin, northwest near Red Rock Canyon.

Disorientation is a constant risk, whether you're searching for your hotel room, stumbling drunkenly through a casino, or desperately trying to remember where you parked the car.

Left Dizzying Strip views from the Stratosphere (p60)

Laugh bawdily as sultry vixens do battle against buff pirates in Sirens of TI (p81) at Treasure Island

>1 STRIP SHOWS

DIVE INTO THE FREE-FOR-ALL ON THE STRIP

The sensory overload of blindingly bright neon lights signifies that yes, you've finally arrived on Las Vegas Blvd (aka the Strip). The infamous Strip has the lion's share of hulking casino hotels and mega-resorts, all flashily competing to lure you (and your wallet) inside. But good news for low rollers: some of the Strip's best stuff is free.

From the beacon shooting toward the stars out of the jet-black pyramid of the Luxor (p49) to the gaudily striped big-top of Circus Circus (p44) to the gigantic Stratosphere Tower (p23), all of the Strip is a spectacle.

No first-time visitor should miss the dancing musical fountains of Bellagio (p80; pictured right), working the illusory magic that a small lake actually exists in the middle of the Mojave Desert.

Just up the street is the Mirage's exploding volcano (p81), recently remodeled to be even bigger and better than it was before.

Meanwhile, next door at TI (Treasure Island), the scantily clad Sirens of TI (p81) face off against hunky beefcake sailors in a hilariously bad, rock 'n' roll battle of the sexes that looks a lot like a Christina Aguilera video.

But that's not all. The opposite side of the Strip holds just as many distractions for freeloaders. Lean over the graceful bridges and balustrades of the Venetian (p62) and watch the singing gondoliers oar their boats through the mock canals of this Italianate casino.

CRUISING THE STRIP

If you're a Vegas first-timer and you're driving, make sure you do a few things. First, arrive after dark. Next, pull over and admire everything from afar. Finally, exit off the interstate and cruise the length of Las Vegas Blvd (aka the Strip). Your eyes will pop out of your head, we bet.

Warning: don't attempt driving the Strip after 9pm on Friday or Saturday night, when weekend traffic will be gridlocked. No wheels? No problem! Ride the double-decker Deuce bus (p190), which runs 24/7 along Las Vegas Blvd. Gray Line (p193) offers a night-time bus tour that lets you gawk at the city's neon lights.

Then hoof it down to Harrah's (p66), where the open-air Carnaval Court (p134) is a free, spring-break party every night, and the 'flair' bartenders juggle fire.

A short walk south is the kitschy Imperial Palace (p66), where 'dealertainers' (p78), dressed like celebrity impersonators (think Elvis, Tina Turner and Billy Idol), put on free song-and-dance shows on the casino floor.

HIGHLIGHTS

>2 ARTS DISTRICT

PARTY WITH THE LOCALS ON FIRST FRIDAY NIGHTS

On the tattered fringes of downtown, hidden among the antique shops and vintage-clothing stores (p88), is the city's emerging 18b Arts District. Drive by it on any given weekday and you might not even notice pivotal landmarks like the Arts Factory (p74; pictured above). But on the first Friday night of each month, these rundown streets take on a carnival atmosphere as 10,000 art lovers, hipsters, indie musicians and hangers-on turn it into one giant block party. Gallery openings, performance art, live music, fortune tellers and tattoo artists are all part of the fun at this fave event of locals. Show up and you might be the only tourist there – a nice change after buzzing around the crowded casinos and megaresorts on the Strip. For celebratory after-party drinks, head to the Beauty Bar (p133).

For more on the local arts scene, see p170.

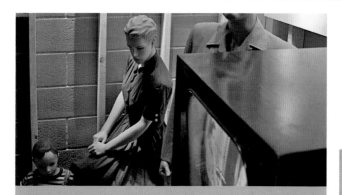

>3 ATOMIC TESTING MUSEUM

EXAMINE THE LEGACY OF THE COLD WAR IN THE DESERT

During the atomic heyday of the 1950s, gamblers and tourists downtown stared mesmerized as mushroom clouds rose behind Fremont St, and the city crowned a Miss Atomic Bomb. Over the next four decades, over 900 nuclear explosions were initiated at the Nevada Test Site, just 65 miles northwest of the city.

Curious to know more? Buy your tickets at the replica of a Nevada Test Site guard station, then spend an hour or two browsing this awesome 8000-sq-ft Smithsonian-affiliated museum (p74). Multimedia exhibits focus on science, technology and the social history of the 'Atomic Age' (p180), which lasted from WWII until atmospheric bomb testing was driven underground in 1961 and a worldwide ban on nuclear testing was declared in 1992. 'Stewards of the Land' galleries examine Southern Nevada's past, present and future, from Native American ways of life to the environmental legacy of atomic testing, including the controversial Yucca Mountain nuclear-waste storage project.

Check out the temporary exhibits of contemporary art and real-life science near the front entrance. Next to them is the cool scientific and retro-minded museum shop, where you can buy your very own A-bomb fallout shelter sign or biohazard T-shirt.

>4 CASINO MEMORABILIA

SHOP FOR ONE-OF-A-KIND GAMBLING SOUVENIRS

As if Las Vegas was ashamed of its own sordid but fascinating history (p179), old-school casinos are being demolished with the speed of a freight train to make room for ever bigger and swankier megaresorts on the Strip. The heyday of outrageous theme hotels is over, too, as one after another, Strip casino hotels trade their gaudy Egyptian gods and faux European landmarks for more chic, but ultimately boring, high-class luxury.

Nothing sticks around for very long in this town. But fans of Old Vegas can still pick up pieces of mobster- and Rat Pack–era casino hotels at fun, funky shops such as Main Street Antiques (p98), which collects vintage casino souvenirs, from Binion's Horseshoe ashtrays and bawdy showgirl brochures to authentic gaming chips from the Dunes and the Sands. Or take home your very own slot machine from Showcase Slots (p99) or a roulette wheel from the Gamblers General Store (p99; pictured above).

Be sure to pay a visit to the 1940s and '50s casino hotels still standing on the Strip, such as the Sahara (p59) and the Tropicana (p69), to snap up logo souvenirs from the gift shop and filch cocktail swizzle sticks and free match books from the bar before these places also go the way of the imploded Stardust and New Frontier.

For more tips on finding vintage Las Vegas, see p176.

>5 CIRQUE DU SOLEIL

JOIN THE AUDIENCE OF AN AVANT-GARDE CIRCUS

During the heyday of the 'Fabulous Fifties,' the Dunes caused a delectable scandal by inviting bare-breasted showgirls to star in its show *Minsky Goes to Paris;* the Stardust imported real French showgirls the next year to star in its topless revue *Lido de Paris*. Both of those legendary casino hotels have since been demolished, and although topless revues still sell out on the Strip – think Bally's *Jubilee!* (p145) and the MGM Grand's Crazy Horse Paris (p145) – today it's Cirque du Soleil shows that rule the roost.

From the bizarre clown antics of Mystère (p147; pictured above), the Strip's longest-running Cirque spectacular (since 1993), the aquatic sensation O at the Bellagio (p40), the martial arts–inspired moves of Kà (p146) and the psychedelic musical journey of LOVE (p147), the troupe's tribute to the Beatles, Québec-born Cirque du Soleil seems tailor-made for Las Vegas, where spectacle is craved above all else. Whimsical multicolored costumes, high-flying aerial acrobatics and giant-sized taiko drums add up to an electrifying atmosphere, and you can easily get caught up in the heart-pounding, sometimes scintillating, but ultimately silly shows.

If you can't score tickets to a Cirque show (they're almost always sold out in advance), drop by Cirque's Revolution Lounge (p154) to get a taste of the fun-for-all carnival atmosphere.

>6 FIRESIDE LOUNGE

REFUEL LATE-NIGHT AT A RETRO STRIPSIDE HIDEAWAY

Booze, bodacious bodies and booty are what many come to Vegas for, in which case a drunken crawl along the Strip is just what the witch doctor ordered.

The launching pad of choice for a wild Vegas night is an ultra lounge (p153), where cocktails are mixed tableside by models, eye-popping go-go dancers shimmy or sky-high views are the specialty of the house. But these are mere stepping stones to Vegas' nightclubs (p142), which are pure fantasyland environments where sin is back in style.

But when it's 4am and your feet hurt after shakin' your booty all night long, where are you gonna go? Escape all of the other tourists at the Peppermill casino's 24-hour Fireside Lounge (p134). Hidden on the North Strip, this pint-sized coffee shop, with its candy-bright neon lights and faux flickering fireplaces, is a beacon.

Take your lover by the hand and step inside, where the swingin' 1970s never ended. Here cooing couples nestle into low-lying couches to make out as they sip exotically colored tropical drinks. The psychedelic decor and special-effects water fountains will be almost as distracting as your cocktail waitress's slinky dress.

Before you know it, the sun will be breaking over Las Vegas Blvd: the perfect end to a wild night.

>7 FREMONT STREET

LET IT ALL HANG OUT IN DOWNTOWN'S HISTORIC GLITTER GULCH

When you've tired of the glitz of the Strip, ride the double-decker Deuce bus (p190) downtown to Fremont St. There you'll discover the city's original hurly-burly casino row, nicknamed Glitter Gulch. This old-school gambling ghetto sprang up beside the railroad tracks back in 1905, more than 40 years before Bugsy cruised down the highway from LA to build the Strip.

Although downtown gambling halls aren't glamorous like Vegas' megaresorts, their proximity to one another is a real plus. Even if you're drunk out of your gourd, you can easily stumble between half a dozen gaming joints here. Play the penny slots, munch a bunch of deep-fried Oreos and Twinkies, grab a 99¢ electric-blue-colored margarita in a 3ft-high plastic glass and buy a tacky T-shirt from a 'Sin City' souvenir shop, while the Fremont Street Experience's cheesy laser-light show (p80) flashes overhead.

The Strip can keep its high-limit poker rooms, VIP velvet ropes and million-dollar shopping arcades – here, everyone can afford to live like the King.

>8 LIBERACE MUSEUM

MAKE A PILGRIMAGE TO A SHRINE OF KITSCH

Known throughout the world as 'Mr Showmanship,' Liberace was awarded six gold records and garnered two stars on the Hollywood Walk of Fame. Following his death in 1987, just a few months after his final public performance at New York's Radio City Music Hall, the late great entertainer was honored by the creation of this outrageous museum (p79) off the Strip.

While audiences enjoyed listening to Liberace's exuberant keyboard artistry, they were also amazed and secretly amused by his outlandish style: priceless pianos, like a rhinestone-encrusted Baldwin and a concert grand covered in mirrors; glittering Rolls-Royces and other exotic cars used to make stage entrances and exits; and fabulous million-dollar furs, feathered capes and sequined suits that are as frighteningly odd as they are funny.

You'll enjoy it all more if you time your visit to coincide with one of the free guided tours led by mad 'Red Hatter' fans, during which no mention will be made of Liberace's homosexuality, his death of AIDS-related complications or the more creepily bizarre rumors that he had his lover (who also happened to be his bodyguard and chauffeur) undergo plastic surgery in order to make him look more like Liberace himself.

>9 MANDALAY BAY BEACH

LAZE BY THE POOL ALL DAY

Las Vegas thrives on a pop culture of excess. Ever since Steve Wynn launched the fabulous Polynesian-themed Mirage casino hotel at the end of the no-holds-barred, money-rules-everything 1980s, every megaresort has aimed to be the biggest and best.

That also applies to resort swimming pools. Despite daunting competition from other casino hotels – such as Caesars Palace (p43), where goddesses proffer frozen grapes in summer, and downtown's Golden Nugget (p47), which has a water slide that shoots swimmers through a glass-enclosed shark tank – the city's most impressive guests-only pool complex is at Mandalay Bay (p50).

'M-Bay' imported 2700 tons of Southern Californian sand to build its artificial beach, where board-riders surf on 6ft-high artificial waves. Grab an inner tube and float away on a 'lazy river' ride, or rent a beachfront cabana or private villa and be royalty for a day. There's an air-conditioned beachside casino, where you can while away the hottest part of the day playing blackjack, roulette and craps. Concerts under the stars hit the beach in summer, when the Miami-inspired Moorea Beach Club attracts sybaritic crowds with its DJs and topless sunbathing. What more could you desire?

For a roundup of Vegas' coolest adults-only pool parties and topless poolside ultra lounges, see the boxed text (p154).

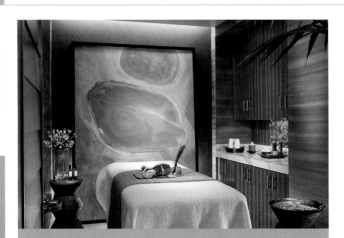

>10 QUA BATHS & SPA
INDULGE IN BODILY BLISS AT A MODERN OASIS

Now more than ever, visiting Las Vegas is not merely about gambling. A stopover in Sin City these days is all about the headlong, hedonistic pursuit of pleasure in all its endless varieties, and so it was inevitable that fantastic, over-the-top spas would blossom like wildflowers here.

Seeking Hawaiian lomilomi, Japanese shiatsu or Thai massage? A volcanic mud or banana-leaf body wrap, a coconut-crème exfoliation? Or how about a lotus-flower bath or a soak in signature apothecary elixirs? At Caesars Palace, Qua Baths & Spa (p149) has everything you desire, and then some. Sweat out your hangover inside the aromatic cedar sauna. Take a dip in the Roman baths. Chill in the arctic room, where dry-ice snowflakes fall. Recline in the exotic-tea lounge, made for socializing with the girls. In the 'Men's Zone,' bad-boy poker players can get a royal shave or have their sore muscles kneaded just like victorious gladiators.

So, what are you waiting for? Treat yourself like an empress or emperor. For more highly recommended spas, see p148.

>11 STRATOSPHERE TOWER

GET HIGH OVER 100 STORIES ABOVE THE STRIP

After a long day traipsing up and down the Strip, especially when the dog days of summer make you sweat, there's no better heat relief than to whoosh up the Stratosphere Tower inside the USA's fastest elevators. There, almost 1150ft above the ground, strong winds make the city's air cooler, not to mention clearer. On a good day, it's a cinch to see for miles across the desert valley encircled by jagged mountains.

Whether you show up for sunset or star gazing, nothing tops this vista. Taking in the eagle's-eye city skyline will make you feel as rich as a high roller, especially while you knock back stiff martinis at the Romance at Top of the World lounge (p137), or fork into a juicy steak at Top of the World restaurant (p115).

But those aren't the only ways to get high atop the Stratosphere Tower. At the pinnacle of the city's tallest building are some adrenaline-pumping thrill rides (p84), including the aptly named Insanity, which swings riders out over the edge of the tower into thin air, then spins 'em round. Or try the Big Shot, which really gets the blood rushing by rocketing riders up and down a steel spire piercing the very top of the tower.

See p84 for more information.

>12 SPRINGS PRESERVE

DISCOVER REAL LIFE IN THE SOUTHERN NEVADA DESERT

Spread over 180 acres atop the site of the original springs and *las vegas* (the meadows), where Southern Paiute tribespeople and Old Spanish Trail traders once pitched their camps, and later Mormon missionaries and Western pioneers settled the Las Vegas Valley, this $250-million museum complex (p76) takes visitors on an incredible trip through historical, cultural and biological time.

If you want to dig beneath the hard-scrabble surface of this desert oasis, start with the OriGen Experience. The 'Natural Mojave' galleries simulate flash floods and expose the variety of native wildlife that call this desert home, from Gila monsters to big brown bats. The 'People of the Springs' exhibit traces the city's obscure history, from Native American dwellings to the arrival of the railroad on the Western frontier and the construction of Hoover Dam. The 'New Frontier' rooms are stocked with kid-friendly interactive multimedia games that teach about conservation, the environment and life in the modern city. Who knew slot machines could be so educational?

The touchstone of the Springs Preserve is the forward-thinking Desert Living Center. Here, Nevada's first platinum-certified LEED

(Leadership in Energy and Environmental Design) buildings stand proudly, constructed of recycled materials and rammed-earth walls, with passive cooling, renewable heating, reclaimed water and solar-electricity panels, all harvesting clean energy. Inside the center are classrooms, learning labs and public exhibits designed to inspire visitors to consider the future of the Strip's neon jungle. The reality is, the sustainability of this fragile desert environment is a huge concern. We think Al Gore would agree – it's an inconvenient truth that can no longer be ignored.

Emerging from the main buildings, outdoor xeriscaped gardens flourish with over 30,000 plants.

Out back more than two miles of walking trails feature interpretive displays that piece together Nevada's cultural and natural history; bring along plenty of water and don't attempt to walk the trails in the blazing midday sun.

Afterward, stop by the nature-themed gift shop, which sells gifts, books, toys and brain-teaser souvenirs. Upstairs is the healthy, eco-conscious Café Wolfgang Puck. The Springs Preserve is also the future home of the Nevada State Museum, which should relocate here in 2009.

For more about Las Vegas' 'green' outlook, see p173.

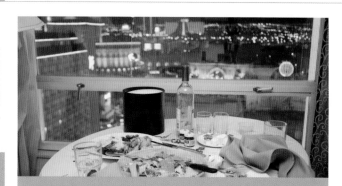

>13 YOUR HOTEL ROOM

HIDE OUT ALL WEEKEND LONG

Sometimes the best thing to do in Las Vegas is absolutely nothing at all – that is, if it's in the deluxe cocoon of your own hotel room or, better yet, a sweeter suite.

Sleeping in late is required for party animals who are out gambling and making merry mayhem till dawn. You'll find hotel rooms here have the most creative (and temptingly collectible) 'Do Not Disturb' signs: the ones at TI (Treasure Island) spell out 'inTImacy requested,' while the MGM Grand's West Wing simply says 'Recharging.'

There's very little that's not available in a minibar or on a room-service menu somewhere in this city. At the Hard Rock (p48), you can order Love Jones lingerie and erotic play boxes (with massage oils and…whoa, handcuffs!) delivered straight to your room. Buckets of champagne on ice are available at almost every casino hotel, but how many will deliver a $6000 combo meal of a burger, French fries and a vintage bottle of Bordeaux straight to your room like at the Palms (p55)?

The plushest casino hotels in Vegas (think Palazzo, Venetian, Wynn Las Vegas, MGM Grand, Caesars Palace and Bellagio) have exclusive all-suites towers staffed with VIP concierges to pamper you with any imaginable amenity, making sure you'll never want to leave.

For advice on where to stay, see p164.

Ship ahoy! The swashbuckling setting of TI (Treasure Island; p61)

ITINERARIES

Although the house always has an edge in Las Vegas, it's a sure bet that there is more to do on the Strip, in downtown and all around town than you'll have time to spare, so make every second count. These high-voltage itineraries will help you get started, fast.

ONE DAY

Speed from the airport to the Strip. Check in at your hotel resort, or just drop off your bags, then go straight to the gaming tables. Take in the Strip's fabulous free attractions (p80) and shopping arcades (p92) as you stroll through opulent megaresorts (p32) such as the Bellagio, Caesars Palace, Venetian, Palazzo and Wynn Las Vegas. Use the monorail (p190) or double-decker Deuce buses (p190) to roll up and down Las Vegas Blvd. Dine at a top chef's table (p104), then party at Sin City's hottest bars (p132) and nightclubs (p142) until the sun comes up. After a quick cat nap, hit a big buffet (see p171) before catching your flight out.

ONE WEEKEND

Fly into Vegas on Friday. Follow the one-day itinerary, but without rushing around like such a crazy person. Fire up your first night at the Strip's ultra lounges (p153) and wind it down around dawn at an after-hours hot spot (p153).

Sleep late the next morning. Laze by the pool (p154), take a gambling lesson or indulge at a primo spa (p148). Get your kicks atop the Stratosphere Tower (p23) as the sun sinks below the horizon, then head downtown to neon-lit Glitter Gulch or boomerang right back to the Strip.

Wake up to an indulgent Sunday brunch (see the boxed text, p126), then gamble or shop like mad until the last minute (even at the airport).

THREE DAYS

Do everything we've recommended in the one-day and one-weekend itineraries. Make time for a trip out of town, too, either to the awe-inspiring Grand Canyon (p156) or nearby Hoover Dam (p158), followed by a scenic drive around Lake Mead and the Valley of Fire. On your last

---

Left The crowds snap away while the big cats slumber at MGM Grand's lion habitat (p77)

day, stop by a half-price ticket booth (see the boxed text, p131) for tickets to a comedy or magic act (p138) or, if you're lucky, a knockout stage show (p144). In the afternoon, detour off the beaten tourist path to the Springs Preserve (p76), Atomic Testing Museum (p74) or downtown's fun, funky 18b Arts District (p14).

COMP CITY

When you're down to the felt (ie on your last dime), don't despair. Some of Las Vegas' best diversions don't cost a thing. Popular low-roller attractions include the Bellagio's dancing fountains (p80), the Mirage's exploding volcano (p81), the Sirens of TI pirate battle at Treasure Island (p81), the MGM Grand's lion habitat (p77), the Flamingo's tropical wildlife gardens (p77), high-wire circus acts at Circus Circus (p80) and celebrity impersonators inside the Imperial Palace casino (p78). Downtown has the unabashedly tacky Fremont Street Experience (p80) and raucous First Friday (p14) block parties. Venture east of the Strip to the Hard Rock casino (p48), where priceless rock 'n' roll memorabilia adorns the walls.

HIGH ROLLERS

Cruise the Strip in a cherry-red convertible and hit the high-stakes poker tables for a taste of James Bond–style action. After sunset, dine with a powerhouse chef (p104), then mingle with Hollywood celebrities at a

Flash the cash at the upmarket Forum Shops (p92)

FORWARD PLANNING

One to six months before you go Book your flights (p188) and accommodations (p164). If you'll be taking any trips out of town (p155), reserve a rental car (p190).

Three to four weeks before you go Start surfing some key Las Vegas websites (see p192) and dabbling in the local media (p193); score tickets for any major concerts, production shows or sporting events that catch your eye (see the boxed text, p151); book a table at a star chef's restaurant (p101).

A week before you go Call your hotel (p164) to check if room prices have dropped and, if they have, request that your reservation rate be lowered, too – you can save hundreds of dollars that way. Make an appointment at one of the Strip's unisex spas (p148) or reserve an out-of-town adventure tour (p161).

The day before you go Reconfirm your flight, hotel and car-rental reservations, and print out copies of everything. Check online (p192) to find out late-breaking news about the hottest nightclubs and live entertainment, then get loads of extra sleep – after you arrive in Sin City, you'll desperately need it!

sultry ultra lounge (p153) and party till dawn in a nightclub's VIP room (p142). Wake up around noon the next day. Start off with a champagne buffet (see p171), then soak up the desert sun by a sexy pool lounge (p154) or luxuriate at a spa (p148). Get your photo taken in a Ferrari at the Exotic Cars showroom at Caesars Palace (p97) after bagging the latest fashions from Milan, Paris and Tokyo inside the Strip's megaresort malls (p92). Peep at a burlesque show after dark (p153).

INDIE VEGAS

When you've tired of the Strip's neon nights, the flip side of Las Vegas beckons. East of Fremont St's casino row is downtown's break-out entertainment district, anchored by the indie Beauty Bar (p133) and hepcats' Downtown Cocktail Room (p134). During daylight hours, wander the 18b Arts District (p14), full of creative art galleries (p74), antiques shops (p95) and only-in-Vegas stores (p98). Find refreshment at locals' fave Luv-It Frozen Custard (p120), then go green at the inspiring Springs Preserve (p76), with its top-notch museum, interpretive trails and gardens, or get a blast of Nevada's atomic past at the Atomic Testing Museum (p74). For sheer silliness, drop by the Pinball Hall of Fame (p79). Time your visit to join up with a First Friday (p14) party or the Vegoose (p132) arts and music festival.

>CASINOS & GAMBLING

Take a chance on lady luck in Las Vegas

CASINOS & GAMBLING

You're on your umpteenth martini. You've just won big the last three hands. Adrenaline pumping, you double down – and lose half of your piggy bank. It's all part of the Vegas experience, and the thrill of hitting the jackpot (no matter how unlikely) is why so many people keep coming back.

It's important to remember one thing: the house advantage. In every game except poker, the house has a statistical winning edge (the 'percentage') over the gambler, and for nearly every payout in nearly every game, the house 'holds' a small portion of the winnings. Amounts vary with the game and with individual bets, but over the long haul, you're guaranteed to lose everything that you gamble. Have fun, but understand the games you're playing, don't bet more than you're prepared to lose, and learn to leave when you're 'up' (ahead).

Traditional casino games include poker, blackjack, baccarat, craps, roulette and slot machines. You must be at least 21 years old to play or even hang around in a casino. Every game has its own customs, traditions and strategies. Almost all casinos hand out written guides to show how to play the game and may offer free one-hour lessons in table games, from Texas Hold'em and blackjack to dice-rollin' craps, all taught by pros. It's OK to ask your dealer for help and advice. For instance, the dealer can tell you what the strategy is for the blackjack hand you've just been dealt. It's polite to 'toke' (tip) the dealer if you are winning. Either place a chip on the layout (the area where you place your bet) for the dealer to take, or place a side bet for the dealer to collect if it wins.

If you play table games seriously, ask the pit boss to rate your play, based on how much you bet and how many hours you play. Las Vegas

---

Top left Why sit bar-side at the Flamingo (p46) when you can nurse your drink in the pool? **Top right** Dress to impress at The Bank (p142) at Bellagio **Bottom** Do your best to imitate the good-luck statues at Harrah's (p66)

casinos give out millions of dollars in 'comps' to rated players (unrated players get nothing) every year.

Even if you're only betting $5 to $10 per hand, you could earn yourself a free buffet pass. Slot-machine and video-poker players earn comps by signing up for casinos' players' clubs. Member-

BEST CASINOS FOR HIGH-LIMIT GAMING
> Bellagio (p40)
> Mansion at MGM Grand (p51)
> Mirage (p52)
> Venetian (p62)
> Wynn Las Vegas (p63)

ship is free, but you must be at least 21 years old and have photo identification. Just go to the players' club desk or the cashier's cage inside the casino and ask to join. You'll have your slot-club card – plus a free souvenir T-shirt, two-for-one show tickets or other welcome gift – within minutes.

POKER

Poker has become the hottest game in town. Fueled by seemingly endless TV coverage and the explosion of online play, would-be legends are flocking to the tables, ready to test their cunning and grit against other hometown heroes and touring pros. Hit a big-league poker room at the wrong time on a Friday night, and you may be in for a three-hour wait just to sit down. Newer, flashier poker rooms have electronic signboards and hand-out pagers to notify you when your seat is available. Nonsmoking rooms are catching on, too.

Many poker rooms take only a small percentage of each pot, leaving the vast majority of the money to be won and lost by the players themselves. Poker betting comes in three basic flavors: limit, no-limit and pot limit. While it's not the only game in town, Texas Hold'em (p175) is far and away the most common. Novices can pick up a strategy book or two from the Gamblers Book Shop (p90).

BLACKJACK

While poker may be grabbing the headlines, blackjack (aka '21') remains far and away the most popular table game Vegas has to offer. Players love blackjack for all kinds of reasons. It's relatively simple to master its basic strategies, and there's easy camaraderie with sociable dealers. Almost every player has had the experience of making an absolute killing at the table, leading them to feel blackjack is a 'beatable' game. But not all blackjack games are created equal, and every casino lays down its own set of rules. Avoid games that won't allow you to split aces or that pay 6:5 odds instead of the usual 3:2.

Nearly all blackjack strategies revolve around one basic fact: because so many cards have a value of 10 – the tens, jacks, queens and kings make up nearly a third of the deck – it's usually good practice to assume that any unknown card, ie the dealer's hole card or the card you are thinking about hitting for, is going to be worth 10. Many gift shops in Las Vegas casino hotels sell little plastic cards telling you what your most advantageous play is in each situation, and friendly dealers will offer you the same advice.

BACCARAT

Nothing conjures the image of high stakes, black tuxedoes and James Bond like baccarat, and yet, of the card games, it possesses the least strategy – none, in fact. The rules of the game are fixed, and there are no decisions for the player except for how to bet. High minimum bets ensure that only those with large bankrolls sit down to play. However, you may be able to find a few mini baccarat tables with $5 minimum bets.

CRAPS

A lively and fast-paced craps table has players shouting, crowds gathering and everyone hoping for that lucky 'hot' streak of the dice. Even

BEST BETS FOR PLAYERS

> Blackjack – Rules vary from table to table, but check out low-roller casinos downtown and on the North Strip.
> Craps – The odds may change, but good times roll at the Strip's Casino Royale, downtown's Main Street Station and Sam's Town off-Strip.
> Race and sports books – Hilton has the world's largest, but Caesars Palace and the MGM Grand are impressive. Bally's by the monorail station is for quick-and-dirty bets.
> Roulette – Paris Las Vegas and the Stratosphere have some of the USA's only authentic European wheels, which improves your odds of winning.
> Video poker – The Palms, west of the Strip, and downtown's Main Street Station usually have full-pay machines.

though the odds are exactly the same on every roll, that doesn't stop people from betting their 'hunches' and believing that certain numbers are 'due.'

Because the betting possibilities are complicated, and shift as play continues, it's important to spend some time studying a betting guide and begin playing with the simplest wager, on the pass/don't pass line, which also happens to be one of the better bets in a Vegas casino.

ROULETTE

The ancient game of roulette is easy to understand and hypnotic to play. Roulette provides the most clear demonstration of the house edge. The roulette wheel has 38 numbers – from 1 to 36, plus 0 and 00 (European roulette wheels typically do not have '00,' which makes the American version much harder). The layout of the wheel is marked with the numbers and various betting combinations.

Most bets pay off at even money, but the chances of a win are less than 50%, because the 0 and 00 don't count as odd or even, red or black, high or low. These aren't the best odds in the casino, but they're far from the worst.

SPEAK LIKE A GAMBLING SAVANT
all in – to bet everything you've got
ante – a starting wager required to play table games
comps – freebies (eg buffet passes, show tickets, hotel rooms) given to players
cooler – an unlucky gambler who makes everyone else lose
dealertainer – a card dealer with an act (eg impersonating Billy Idol)
eye in the sky – high-tech casino surveillance systems
fold – to throw in your cards and stop betting
high roller – a gambler who bets big (aka 'whale')
let it ride – to roll over a winning wager into the next bet
low roller – a small-time gambler (eg likes 1¢ slot machines)
marker – IOU credit-line debt owed to a casino
one-armed bandit – old-fashioned nickname for a slot machine
pit boss – a card dealer's supervisor on the casino floor
sucker bet – a gamble on nearly impossible odds
toke – a tip or gratuity

SLOT MACHINES & VIDEO POKER

Simplest of all are slot machines – just put in money and pull the handle (or push a button) – and they're wildly popular. A player can have no effect on the outcome. The probabilities are programmed into the machine, and the chances of winning (or more likely losing) are the same on every pull.

Some machines pay back a higher proportion of the money deposited than others; those with larger-than-average returns (up to 98%) are called 'loose.'

If you hit the jackpot, always wait by the machine until an attendant arrives, so you can claim your prize.

Popular with locals, video poker games are often built into a bar. By employing correct strategy (math whizzes can memorize strategy tables) and finding machines with the best payout schedules, it's possible to improve your chances of winning.

Look for machines that reward a pair of jacks or better, and have a one-coin payout of nine coins for a full house and six coins for a flush (ie a 9/6 Jacks or Better machine).

SPORTS BOOKS

The bigger casinos usually have a race and sports book, a room where major sports events are televised. Players can bet on just about any game, boxing match or horse race in the country, except for those taking place in Nevada.

Race and sports books are best during major events, when everyone is captivated by, betting on and yelling about the same thing, such as NFL Monday Night Football, college basketball's March Madness and pro baseball's World Series.

MAJOR PLAYERS & GAMBLING-HALL FAVES

Las Vegas literally has scores of casinos, all offering different games and odds.

The following pages describe major players on Las Vegas Blvd and downtown's Fremont St, plus a few other gambling-hall faves, both on and off the Strip. All are open 24 hours, don't charge admission, are wheelchair-accessible and offer free self-service and valet parking (tip at least $2).

BELLAGIO

Built by Steve Wynn on the site of the legendary Dunes, the **Bellagio** (☎ 693-7111; www.bellagio.com; 3600 Las Vegas Blvd S; Ⓜ Bally's/Paris) is Vegas' original, opulent, if entirely parvenu, pleasure villa. You may recognize it from the 2001 remake of the Rat Pack–era movie *Ocean's Eleven*. At the water's edge of an artificial lake, from which spring more than a thousand dancing fountains (p80), is a cluster of Tuscan buildings purporting the illusion of having been plucked from Italy's Lake District.

Although the nouveau-riche stink can be heady, the secret delight of the Bellagio is that romance is always in the air, and natural light swathes plenty of private nooks where you can soak up the atmosphere. Beyond the glass-and-metal *porte cochere* you'll find a stable of high-end restaurants (p102), a swish shopping concourse (p94), a fine-art gallery (p74) and a European-style casino.

The hotel's gasp-worthy lobby is adorned with Dale Chihuly's glass sculpture composed of 2000 hand-blown flowers in vibrant colors. Real flowers, cultivated in a gigantic on-site greenhouse, brighten countless vases throughout the property and an over-the-top conservatory (p77). In the courtyard, a swimming pool is accented by carved Italian columns and manicured citrus and parterre gardens.

Baby strollers and unaccompanied children under 18 are not allowed at the Bellagio.

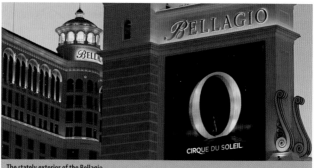
The stately exterior of the Bellagio

David Williams
Poker pro with a World Series of Poker championship bracelet and a sweet Strip-view condo

How'd you get started playing cards? I grew up in a gambling household. Both my grandfather and my mother played cards. **Why poker, not blackjack or another game?** Poker is the only game where skill matters. Over time, good players win. **Your poker success – is it luck or smarts?** I'm a math person, so I know luck all evens out. I've had my bad days, too. Success comes from patience, practice and dedication. **Why is no-limit Texas Hold'em your favorite game?** It's the most popular, and the most lucrative. Anyone knows it, and everyone plays it. **Top casino poker rooms?** Bellagio (opposite) and Venetian (p62). **How to keep cool when you're betting millions of dollars** I get so caught up in winning, in the competition of it all, that the money becomes irrelevant.

BINION'S

The ex-Horseshoe casino was opened in 1951 by notorious Texan gambler Benny Binion, who sported gold coins for buttons on his cowboy shirts. In the Vegas tradition of one-upmanship, **Binion's** (☎ 382-1600; www .binions.com; 128 E Fremont St; 🚌 Deuce) once offered punters a chance to drool over $1 million worth of gold certificates kept in a glass display case shaped, appropriately enough, like a lucky horseshoe.

It was Binion who oversaw the transformation of downtown's Fremont St from a row of sawdust gambling halls into 'Glitter Gulch,' where classy carpet joints gave away free drinks to slot players and sent limos to the airport for high-rollin' whales. A savvy horse trader, Binion once quipped 'An honest deal makes its own friends.' His casino became best known for its 'zero limit' betting policy, and as the place where the World Series of Poker was born.

Now that Benny has gone to the great round-up in the sky, his namesake casino is struggling to live up to its legacy. Despite being a slightly rundown and diminutive downtown gambling hall, Binion's retains its larger-than-life standing among Strip casino giants, and the gaming tables are filled day and night. It's worth swinging by this country-and-western-flavored casino's high-stakes poker room to witness nail-biting, around-the-clock Texas Hold'em action.

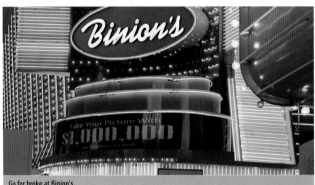

Go for broke at Binion's

CAESARS PALACE

As showcased in the Hollywood film *Rain Man*, **Caesars Palace** (☎ 731-7110; www.caesarspalace.com; 3570 Las Vegas Blvd S; Ⓜ Flamingo/Caesars Palace) upped the luxury ante for the gaming industry when it debuted in the 1960s. The Greco-Roman fantasyland captured the world's attention with its full-size marble reproductions of classical statuary, its Stripside row of towering fountains and its cocktail waitresses costumed as goddesses.

Thanks to ongoing megabucks renovations, Caesars is redefining its swanky self. At the sybaritic Garden of the Gods Oasis pool complex, hotties proffer frozen grapes in summer, and topless sunbathing is allowed at the Venus pool. Pure (p144) nightclub and the Pussycat Dolls Lounge (p153) are celeb-happy nightspots.

Although Caesars appears poised to rule the empire once again, the Palace remains quintessentially kitschy Vegas. Bar girls continue to roam the gaming areas in skimpy togas, and the fountains are still out front – the same ones daredevil Evil Knievel made famous when he jumped them on a motorcycle on December 31, 1967.

Two imperial casinos contain more than 100 card tables and a couple of thousand slots that will accept up to $500 chips, as well as a race and sports book with giant TV screens. Fashionistas saunter inside the upscale Forum Shops (p92), which feature an aquarium and bizarre animatronic fountain shows. The Colosseum, a 4100-seat showroom modeled after its Roman namesake, puts on lavish theatrical spectacles. Also found here are a galaxy of star chefs' restaurants (p103).

Bask in the lap of luxury at Caesars Palace

CIRCUS CIRCUS

While cruising the bedraggled North Strip, it's pretty hard to miss **Circus Circus** (☎ 734-0410; www.circuscircus.com; 2880 Las Vegas Blvd S; 🚌 Deuce), what with its enormous clown-shaped marquee and tent-shaped casino under a gaudily striped big top. From the outside, this sprawling resort may look pretty cheesy – and it definitely *is*. It's also overrun with kiddies and baby strollers.

Open since 1968, this casino hotel was originally intended to stand beside Caesars Palace; that way, it could've had a Roman circus theme. But that wasn't meant to be, so now it's just a plain circus here. The decor is a riotous carnival of colors, mainly pinks and oranges, that aims for Ringling Bros more than *commedia dell'arte*. A trio of full-sized casinos have over 2200 slot machines (keep an eye out for those spinning carousels), plus zany table games like 'Casino War.'

If you're a wild child yourself, relive scenes from Hunter S Thompson's gonzo journalism epic *Fear and Loathing in Las Vegas: A Savage Journey to the Heart of the American Dream* here, but even without the drugs it's hallucinogenic enough. Elevated above the casino floor, trapeze artists, high-wire workers, jugglers and unicyclists perform stunts (p80), while out back is the Adventuredome (p81) amusement park. Cacophonous Slots A' Fun (p80) is just a drunken stumble away.

Rediscover your inner child at Circus Circus

EXCALIBUR

Arthurian legends notwithstanding, this medieval caricature, complete with crayon-colored towers and a faux drawbridge, epitomizes gaudy Vegas. **Excalibur** (☎ 597-7777; www.excalibur.com; 3850 Las Vegas Blvd S; Ⓜ MGM Grand) could have resembled an elegant English castle, but its designers decided to go the kitschy route instead, which is just fine with the cheapskate frat boys and families with rambunctious young kids who stay here.

Inside the inane mock-castle, the casino walls are hung with coats of arms and cheap stained-glass art imitations that depict valiant knights and lovely damsels. Down on the Fantasy Faire Midway are buried Ye Olde carnival games like skee-ball, and there are joystick joys and Merlin's Magic Motion Machine ridefilms in the Wizard's Arcade. For kids, the Tournament of Kings dinner show is a demolition derby with hooves and sticky fingers.

Excalibur is handily connected to Luxor by an underground moving walkway. A free tram also links Excalibur, Luxor and Mandalay Bay.

Experience a taste of medieval times at Excalibur

FLAMINGO

In 1946 the **Flamingo** (☎ 733-3111; www.flamingolasvegas.com; 3555 Las Vegas Blvd S;
Ⓜ Flamingo/Caesars Palace) was the talk of the town. The New York mafia
had shelled out millions to finish building this tropical gaming oasis in
the desert. Billy Wilkerson, owner of the *Hollywood Reporter* and some
sizzling-hot LA nightclubs, originally broke ground here. But he ran out of
money fast, so the mob stepped in.

It was prime gangster Americana, initially managed by the infamous
mobster Benjamin 'Bugsy' Siegel, who named it after his girlfriend,
dancer Virginia Hill, called 'The Flamingo' for her red hair and long legs.
Siegel died in a hail of bullets at Hill's Beverly Hills bungalow soon after
the Flamingo opened, the victim of a contract killing. The Flamingo had
gotten off to a rocky start and the investors mistakenly believed it would
ultimately fail, so they 'took care of business.' But they were so wrong:
not only did the Flamingo survive, it kick-started modern Las Vegas and
the entire Strip.

Today, the Flamingo isn't quite what it was back when its janitorial
staff wore tuxedos; think more *Miami Vice*, less *Bugsy*. But it's always
crowded in the casino. Drop by during the madhouse sunset happy hour
to sling back margaritas in souvenir glasses and watch women of ques-
tionable repute stroll past the front doors. Bugsy would've loved it.

Soak up the retro atmosphere at Flamingo

GOLDEN NUGGET

The Golden Nugget's namesake claim to fame is the Hand of Faith. (No, it's not a religious relic.) It's the heftiest hunk of gold ever found, weighing a massive 61lb 11oz. Discovered in Australia, today it's on display under glass near the North Tower elevators. Yet that's not all this bejeweled gambling palace is known for.

When it debuted as the world's largest casino in 1946, the **Golden Nugget** (☎ 385-7111; www.goldennugget.com; 129 E Fremont St; 🚌 Deuce) looked like a million bucks and, unbelievably, poker players were allowed to deal their own cards. In the 1970s, casino impresario Steve Wynn brought vintage Vegas back into style by inviting Frank Sinatra to star at the Theater Ballroom (p140). The enterprising 21st-century wunderkind duo Tim Poster and Thomas Breitling catapulted the Nugget into the national limelight on the Fox reality-TV series *Casino*.

Day or night, the Nugget is downtown's most glam address, although the crowds of polyester-clad retirees are the antithesis of hip. The glittering casino has a spread of table games, notably a cool, nonsmoking poker room. DJs spin at Gold Diggers (p135), live bands rock the RUSH Lounge, old-school steaks are served at Vic & Anthony's (p121) and Italian pizzas are wood-fired at the Grotto (p119). Reserved for hotel guests, a three-story water slide thrillingly plunges through a 200,000-gallon shark tank into a swimming pool outside.

Slide through a shark tank at the Golden Nugget and live to tell the tale

HARD ROCK

The world's first rock 'n' roll casino, the hot, hot, hot **Hard Rock** (☎ 693-5000; www.hardrockhotel.com; 4455 Paradise Rd; 🚌 108, 202) embraces what may be the most impressive collection of rock-star memorabilia ever assembled under one roof. Among the priceless items being watched over by the 'eye in the sky' and eagle-eyed security guards suited up like bouncers are some of the more bodacious fashion statements by Elvis and Britney Spears; a custom motorcycle (donated by Nikki Sixx of Mötley Crüe) that once belonged to the Hell's Angels gang; and Jim Morrison's handwritten lyrics to one of The Doors' greatest hits.

All in all, this sexy, see-and-be-seen scene is perfect for entourage wannabes, and is especially beloved by SoCal partiers. A roomy circular casino has a state-of-the-art race and sports book. Raised above the main casino floor are The Joint (p140), a rock-concert venue, Body English nightclub (p142), ultra-trendy restaurants AGO (p121) and Nobu (p122), and a priceless handful of boutique shops (p93). There's seasonal swim-up blackjack at the Beach Club, which opens to the public for Rehab (see the boxed text, p154) pool parties on smokin' summer Sundays.

Like a shot of Viagra, the Hard Rock's current $750 million expansion project should only enhance the potency of its forever-young appeal.

Take a tour through rock 'n' roll history at the Hard Rock

CASINOS & GAMBLING

LUXOR

Named after Egypt's ancient city perched on the east bank of the Nile, the landmark **Luxor** (☎ 262-4000; www.luxor.com; 3900 Las Vegas Blvd S; 🚌 Deuce) once had the biggest 'wow!' factor of the South Strip's megaresorts. It tenuously hung in the balance between being a pyramid of gaudiness and a refined shrine to Egyptian art, architecture and antiquities. All that kitsch is now going the way of the pharaohs, as a brash North African theme is slowly replaced with sexed-up nightlife and contempo restaurants (p106).

Fronting the 30-story pyramid cloaked in black glass from base to apex is a crouching sphinx and a sandstone obelisk etched with hieroglyphics. For now, the pyramid's interior is stuffed full of enormous Egyptian statues of guards, lions and rams; sandstone columns and walls adorned with tapestries; a stunning replica of the Great Temple of Ramses II; and a pharaoh's treasure of polished marble. The hotel atrium is so voluminous it could fit nine Boeing 747s stacked on top of one another. At the apex of the pyramid, a 40-billion-candlepower beacon, the world's most powerful, sends a shaft of bluish white light 10 miles out into space, where it's visible by astronauts.

The Luxor is linked to Excalibur by an underground moving walkway. To get to Mandalay Bay, walk through Mandalay Place (p93) mall. A free tram also connects Luxor with Mandalay Bay and Excalibur.

Walk like an Egyptian at Luxor

MANDALAY BAY

The tropical-themed '**M-Bay**' (☎ 632-7777; www.mandalaybay.com; 3950 Las Vegas Blvd S; 🚌 Deuce) fails to match the grandeur of Vegas' more famous mega-resorts, although high-stakes gamblers will appreciate a classy casino that seems as limitless as the credit line needed to play here. Everything can be a spectacle here, if you only know where to look.

There's rock-star karaoke at the House of Blues (see the boxed text, p139) entertainment complex, catsuit-clad 'angels' scaling the wine tower at Aureole (p106), and a frozen vodka locker where sable fur coats are lent to members inside Red Square (see the boxed text, p136). Stylish boutique extras include Mandalay Place (p93), a skybridge shopping promenade, and the minimalist modern THEhotel with its lofty Mix bar (p136) and bathhouse spa (p148).

M-Bay's aquatic theme hinges on the Shark Reef (p78), an awesome glassed-in, walk-through aquarium; and the artificial Mandalay Beach, built with 2700 tons of imported Californian sand, featuring summer 'dive-in' movies, surfing competitions in an artificial wave pool, starlight concerts and clothing-optional Moorea Beach Club. If the stress of gambling in the air-con beachside casino gets to be too much, retire to a rooftop cabana or float away on a lazy river ride.

Free trams shuttle between Mandalay Bay and the Luxor and Excalibur casino hotels.

Rock out to live music and maybe belt out a tune of your own at the House of Blues, Mandalay Bay

MGM GRAND

With over 5040 rooms, **MGM Grand** (☎ 891-1111; www.mgmgrand.com; 3799 Las Vegas Blvd S; Ⓜ MGM Grand) retains the 'world's largest hotel' crown, despite mounting competition. Astoundingly, the resort contains no fewer than 18,000 doors, 7778 beds and 93 elevators. The important thing to remember is that despite its enormous size, the shimmering emerald-green 'City of Entertainment' – looking like something straight out of *The Wizard of Oz* – manages to feel intimate, even clubby.

Owned by movie corp Metro Goldwyn Mayer, the MGM has co-opted themes from Hollywood movies, down to the black-and-white photos of yesteryear's film stars hanging in the restrooms. The casino consists of a gigantic, circular room with a domed ceiling and replicated 1930s glamour. The gaming area is equal in size to four football fields and offers a whopping selection of slots and table games, plus a hot poker room next to a race and sports book with VIP skyboxes.

Out front, it's hard to miss the USA's largest bronze statue, a 100,000lb lion that's 45ft tall, perched atop a pedestal ringed by fountains and Atlas-themed statues. More 'Maximum Vegas' attractions include the lion habitat (p77), the gigantic Grand Garden Arena (see the boxed text, p151), which hosts championship boxing bouts and concerts, Cirque du Soleil's martial arts–inspired show Kà (p146), the topless revue Crazy Horse Paris (p145) and a celebrity-chef line-up (p108).

The glittering facade at the MGM Grand

MIRAGE

Despite having been open for more than 20 years, there's still nothing quite like casino mogul Steve Wynn's most exotic creation, **Mirage** (☎ 791-7111; www.mirage.com; 3400 Las Vegas Blvd S; M Harrah's/Imperial Palace). Its paradisiacal tropical setting, replete with an atrium of jungle foliage and waterfalls (p78), captures the imagination. Out front in a lagoon, the fiery trademark faux volcano (p81) erupts nightly, stopping slack-jawed onlookers in their tracks.

The scents of jasmine and vanilla often waft through the hotel lobby. Circling the atrium is a huge Polynesian-themed casino, which incorporates the design concept of placing gaming areas under separate roofs to invoke a feeling of intimacy. Real and faux tropical plants add to the splendor of the casino, which has a high-stakes poker room.

All of that tropical-themed stuff is fast becoming the old Mirage, though. Here the new theme is 'remixed.' Until recently the Mirage had been outstripped by newer, splashier megaresorts, including Steve Wynn's eponymous resort just up the road. But the Mirage is climbing back toward the top of the Strip game after adding a hot nightclub, Jet (p142), the adults-only pool lounge Bare (see the boxed text, p154) and powerhouse eateries (p109).

Although the dynamic duo is no longer performing here, you can still visit Siegfried & Roy's Secret Garden & Dolphin Habitat (p78), then pay your respects to the giant shrine-like bronze statue of the legendary illusionists standing outside on the Strip.

Gaze at the underwater world in the Mirage lobby

NEW YORK–NEW YORK

Give me your tired, huddled (over a Wheel of Fortune slot machine) masses. The mini-megapolis of **New York–New York** (☎ 740-6969; www.nyny hotelcasino.com; 3790 Las Vegas Blvd S; Ⓜ MGM Grand) has scaled-down replicas of the Empire State Building and Statue of Liberty, a mini Brooklyn Bridge and scale-warped renditions of the Chrysler and Ziggurat buildings, all topped off by a Coney Island–style roller coaster (p82) wrapped around the colorful facade. The crowd is young and party-hardy.

Zany design elements throughout reflect NYC's bold color, history and diversity. Don't overlook the Rockefeller restrooms or the USA bas-relief map at America coffee shop. Claustrophobes, beware. This Disneyfied version of the Big Apple can get more crowded than the real deal: around 200,000 pedestrians stride across NYC's Brooklyn Bridge each year, but around 15 million traverse the Vegas version annually.

Slews of slots and gaming tables are set against a rich backdrop of famous landmarks, with high-limit 'Gaming on the Green.' The Bar at Times Square (p132) is famous for its dueling piano acts. Sip a more civilized pint outdoors at Nine Fine Irishmen (see the boxed text, p136), where live Celtic bands play, or taste North American microbrews at Pour 24 (see the boxed text, p136). Sports fans gravitate to ESPN Zone Sports Arena (p82), which has a high-tech video and virtual-reality game arcade upstairs.

Learn a trick or two at Houdini's Magic Shop (p98), New York–New York

PALAZZO

A grandiose sequel to the Venetian (p62), the **Palazzo** (☎ 607-7777; www
.palazzolasvegas.com; 3325 Las Vegas Blvd S; M Harrah's/Imperial Palace) opened opposite Wynn Las Vegas with great fanfare in 2008. This upscale casino
hotel was supposed to have been called Lido, after the Italian island just
a short boat ride away from Venice at the edge of the Andean Sea. Here
in Las Vegas, you can walk from Venice to its offshore island in just a few
minutes.

The Venetian and Palazzo resorts are connected via an interior corridor.
Entering the Palazzo, you'll emerge into an airy, sunshine-filled atrium
with a waterfall feature, a fave photo op for camera-toting tourists.
Soaring 50 floors toward the sky, the Palazzo's all-suites hotel tower is
the city's tallest today. The casino itself measures over 100,000 sq ft, with
the usual spread of high-limit table games and slot and video-poker
machines with less-favorable odds.

At the Shoppes at Palazzo (p94), international designers flaunt their
goodies, while the Canyon Ranch SpaClub (p148) induces aqua-thermal
bliss. High-flying restaurants (p111) include exhilarating ventures by culinary heavyweights Charlie Trotter, Emeril Legasse and Wolfgang Puck.

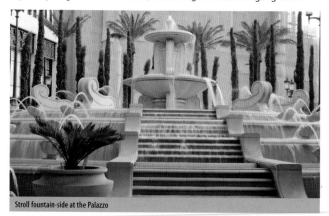

Stroll fountain-side at the Palazzo

PALMS

Designed to seduce Gen-Xers and Gen-Yers, the ultramodern **Palms** (☎ 942-7777; www.palms.com; 4321 W Flamingo Rd; 🚌 202) catapulted into the limelight with a starring role on MTV's *Real World* reality-TV series and Bravo's *Celebrity Poker Showdown*. Today it's Hugh Hefner's Playboy Club that calls the shots, and you'll have to cough up some cash to peek inside his hybrid casino-nightspot atop the Palms' Fantasy Tower, where flashy Moon (p143) nightclub has a retractable roof that opens up to the desert's starry skies.

Downstairs the high-drama, neon-lit atmosphere is equal parts sexy and downright cheesy – just like the Playboy bunnies upstairs. The main casino has quick cocktail service and a heavenly spread of full-pay video poker machines, plus two poker rooms and a race and sports book with interactive TVs and specialty wagering. The first-rate movie theater (p137) hosts the CineVegas film festival (p132).

Other places to see and be seen include Hart & Huntington Tattoo Shop, with its blood-red curtained fortune teller's booth out front; N9NE steakhouse (p127) and towering Alizé (p125) French restaurant; ghostbar (p153), a sky-high ultra lounge that packs in celebs; and The Pearl (p140), a state-of-the-art concert hall and recording studio.

The Palms recently upped the ante with Palms Place, a high-rise condo-style hotel connected to the main complex by the SkyTube, an enclosed moving walkway.

Imbibe a martini or three at the Palms

PARIS LAS VEGAS

Adorned with fake Francophonic signs such as 'Le Car Rental,' the multimillion-dollar Gallic caricature **Paris Las Vegas** (☎ 946-7000; www.parislasvegas.com; 3655 Las Vegas Blvd S; Ⓜ Bally's/Paris) strives to evoke the gaiety of the grand dame by re-creating her famous landmarks, including the Paris Opera House, Arc de Triomphe, Hotel de Ville, Louvre and the River Seine. Just like in the French capital, the signature attraction is the ersatz Eiffel Tower (p82), where visitors can ascend in a glass elevator to a head-spinning observation platform overlooking the Strip.

Surrounded by street scenes from both banks of the Seine, the bustling vault-ceilinged casino, complete with replica Métropolitain arches, is home to almost a hundred gaming tables, a couple of thousand slot machines, a race and sports book and some of the USA's only authentic French roulette wheels (which have no '00') in the high-limit area. Crème de la crème champagne is waiting on ice at Napoleon's bar (p137), not far from the savory-and-sweet La Creperie.

Paris is conveniently connected to Bally's monorail station by a petit shopping arcade, where high heels clack along cobblestone streets.

Magnifique! The grounds of Paris Las Vegas

PLANET HOLLYWOOD

In a slightly out-of-the-way locale, **Planet Hollywood** (☎ 785-5555; www.planet hollywoodresort.com; 3667 Las Vegas Blvd S; Ⓜ Bally's/Paris) took its sweet time stripping the ex-Aladdin casino hotel of all of the trappings of its Middle Eastern fantasy. For fans of vintage Vegas, that felt like a crime. But for Paris Hilton imitators, World Series of Poker wannabes and those who like their casinos pimped out in LA style, the new PH fits the bill.

Dating from the 1950s, the original Aladdin, where Elvis and Priscilla Presley married, was imploded in 1998. Retooled to target the Asian and European jet set, the new Aladdin megaresort opened its doors just two years later. Quickly thereafter the owners made the largest bankruptcy filing ever in Nevada history. Some pundits even speculated that the property was hexed. The Aladdin's *new* new owners have dramatically changed this megaresort. For now, the genie's latest masters have kept a few of the Aladdin's gold-star attractions, including the Spice Market Buffet (p114), while adding new tastebud ticklers like Koi (p114) sushi bar and bordello-esque Strip House (p114) for steaks.

But don't hold your breath: no-one has ever made a mint with this property – not yet, anyway. Your best bet is shopping at the adjacent Miracle Mile Shops (p94), formerly Desert Passage; sipping a masterfully made mai tai at tropical Trader Vic's (p137); and partying after-hours at Krāve nightclub (p143).

Planet Hollywood offers an LA-style experience

RIO

The name of this wildly popular casino hotel says a lot about the **Rio** (☎ 777-7777; www.riolasvegas.com; 3700 W Flamingo Rd; 🚌 free Strip shuttle). The corny Masquerade Village, the center of the action, offers an ongoing *carnaval* atmosphere. In the free 'Show in the Sky,' Mardi Gras floats suspended from tracks in the ceiling parade above the gaming tables while racily costumed performers dance and lip-synch to pop rock and jazzy numbers, and toss shiny beaded necklaces to the crowds. The rambunctious fun is infectious. You can even ride along in one of the floats while having your souvenir photo taken for a fee (reservations required).

Occupying most of the 'village' is an enormous casino decked out with a Brazilian motif, where 'bevertainers' bring around drinks in between doing 90-second song-and-dance numbers. In addition to 80 table games and 1200 slot machines, the Rio's poker room, home to the World Series of Poker (p132), attracts sharks. Ringed around the casino are two of Vegas' best buffets, Carnival World & Village Seafood Buffets (p125). Lucky Strike Lanes is a mod bowling alley where hipsters and frat boys knock back Buds and watch Monday Night Football. After dark, illusionists Penn & Teller (p139) and the Chippendales dancers (see boxed text, p152) entertain the good-time masses.

Cut loose, Latin-style, at the Rio

SAHARA

Standing in the no-man's-land of the North Strip, the **Sahara** (☎ 737-2111; www.saharavegas.com; 2535 Las Vegas Blvd S; Ⓜ Sahara) is a survivor. The Moroccan-themed casino is one of the few vintage Vegas icons to withstand the onslaught of corporate megaresorts. After the Sahara threw open its doors in 1952, its Conga Room showcased everyone from jazz singer Ella Fitzgerald to the Beatles.

The Moroccan theme starts at the Stripside entrance with an arched marble dome shadowed by several dozen royal palms. The *Arabian Nights* theme continues inside the casino, with gold-painted ceilings and molded columns laced with colorful vines, guarded by severe-looking statues of Middle Eastern sultans. The casino hustles the Strip's largest variety of unique card games (which will probably take all of your dough). Outside, Elvis Presley and Elizabeth Taylor once lounged by the swimming pool adorned with Moroccan mosaic tiles.

These days the Sahara is less glamorous than it sounds. Its bread-and-butter crowd is Nascar fans, who knock back bottles of Bud in the Nascar Café, ringed around Carzilla, the world's largest stock car. More compelling for speed freaks are the thrill rides, especially Speed (p83), a roller coaster that loops through the camel marquee sign.

Pretend you're back in the Fabulous '50s at the Sahara

CASINOS & GAMBLING

STRATOSPHERE

Las Vegas has many buildings exceeding 20 stories, but only the **Strato-sphere** (☎ 380-7777; www.stratospherehotel.com; 2000 Las Vegas Blvd S; Ⓜ Sahara) tops a hundred. At 1149ft, the three-legged Stratosphere Tower is the tallest building in the USA west of the Mississippi River. At the base of the tapered tower is a casino favored by a loud-talkin', hard-drinkin' redneck crowd, but with little else in the way of a theme, although it does boast low-limit table games and 1500 reputedly loose slots and video-poker machines.

Atop the Strip's lucky landmark are viewing decks, which afford spectacular 360-degree panoramas; you'll also find a revolving restaurant (p115) and a sophisticated cocktail lounge (p137). To get you there, the tower boasts the USA's fastest elevators, which lift you 108 floors in a mere 37 ear-popping seconds. Once you've recovered from the 20mph vertical rocket ride, jump on the tower's high-altitude thrill rides (p84).

Back down inside the low-roller's casino, you can buy tickets to some of the Strip's cheesiest production shows, like the laughable late-night vampire girlie show *Bite*, then spend the rest of your chump change in the nearby kingdom of kitsch, Bonanza Gifts (p98).

Brace yourselves, thrill seekers! The Stratosphere's rides are 110 stories above the Strip

TI (TREASURE ISLAND)

Yo, ho, whoa: the shift at TI (☎ 894-7111; www.treasureisland.com; 3300 Las Vegas Blvd S; 🚌 Deuce) from family-friendly to bawdy and oh-so-naughty epitomized Vegas' racy efforts to put 'sin' back in 'casino,' starting in the late '90s. Though traces of Treasure Island's original swashbuckling skull-and-crossbones theme linger (if you look hard), the reimagined TI, a terracotta-toned resort that aims to re-create an elegant Caribbean hideaway, practically screams 'leave the kids at home.'

You'll approach the property via a wood-bottomed, hemp-roped bridge that spans the artificial Sirens' Cove, set beside a vague replica of an 18th-century sea village, where the spicy Sirens of TI (p81) show is staged several times nightly, weather permitting. The adults-only theme continues inside the sprawling casino. One-armed Playboy bandits await where plastic chests full-o-booty once reigned. The gaming tables are tightly grouped, but no-one seems to mind – the place is always packed. There's also a huge party-friendly hot tub, the tequila goddess at Isla Mexican Kitchen (p115) and a Strip-view patio for late-night noshes at Social House (p116).

Easing the journey here and back is a free tram shuttling gamblers to the Mirage next door. So, now you've got a handy alibi when stopping by for a quick squeeze – of the slot-machine handles, of course.

Seek your bounty at TI (Treasure Island)

VENETIAN

Casino impresario Sheldon Adelson broke ground on his replica of La Repubblica Serenissima (Most Serene Republic) – reputed to be the home of the world's first casino – shortly after the controversial and dramatic implosion of the vintage Sands casino hotel in 1996. On this hallowed ground, the Rat Pack frolicked; this was where Frank Sinatra, Dean Martin, Sammy Davis Jr and the rest of the gang hobnobbed with movie stars, senators and showgirls during the 'Fabulous Fifties.' When the Sands tumbled down, a piece of the city's history was lost.

Inspired by the splendor of Italy's most-romantic city, the luxury mega-resort **Venetian** (☎ 414-1000; www.venetian.com; 3355 Las Vegas Blvd S; Ⓜ Harrah's/Imperial Palace) boasts reproductions of Venetian landmarks including the doge's palace, *campanile* (bell tower), St Mark's Sq and even a mini Rialto Bridge with an ahistorical escalator added. Graceful bridges, flowing canals, vibrant piazzas and stone walkways faithfully imitate the Venetian spirit, especially inside the Grand Canal Shoppes (p93), where gondolas (p84) set sail. Poker pros play high-stakes, no-limit Texas Hold'em inside the spacious casino. More mega-attractions include sultry Tao (p144) nightclub; the world-class Canyon Ranch SpaClub (p148) and fitness center; and top-drawer gourmet restaurants (p116), some with star chefs confidently at the helm.

The Venetian is linked to neighboring Palazzo (p54) via the Grand Canal Shoppes.

Sample la dolce vita at the Venetian

WYNN LAS VEGAS

Instead of an exploding volcano or an Eiffel tower out front to lure the crowds, legend Steve Wynn's eponymous resort **Wynn Las Vegas** (☎ 770-7000; www.wynnlasvegas.com; 3145 Las Vegas Blvd S; 🚍 Deuce) is all about exclusivity – step inside so you can snub the hoi polloi flooding Las Vegas Blvd, secure in your lavish retreat. VIPs who reserve a suite even get to use a private side entrance.

Perhaps the most remarkable thing about Wynn is the painstaking attention to detail. It's as if the Mirage and Bellagio were Wynn's rough drafts. Elements of both of the mogul's former projects peek through here. The decor recalls the Bellagio, but with more vibrant colors and in-laid flower mosaics. Lush greenery recalls the Mirage, but with panoramic windows, natural light and al-fresco seating at every turn.

The signature copper-toned resort (literally speaking, Wynn's name is written in script across the top, punctuated by a period) is shielded from the Strip by an artificial 'mountain.' Gawking tourists cross over footbridges into the resort, waltzing by the Ferrari/Maserati dealership, haute-couture shops of Wynn Esplanade (p95) and sumptuous restaurants (p117). Inside the enormous casino is a popular poker room attracting pros around the clock, slot machines from a penny up to $5K per pull, a mammoth race and sports book and a spread of mostly high-minimum table games.

Fine dining awaits at Wynn Las Vegas' restaurant Alex (p117)

OTHER CASINOS

BALLY'S

☎ 739-4111; www.ballyslasvegas.com; 3645 Las Vegas Blvd S; Ⓜ Bally's/Paris

Unless it's 'bigger is better,' there's no real theme at the Strip's most staid megaresort, with a football field–sized casino overhung by twinkling chandeliers and overstuffed blue-velvet chairs. But Bally's biggest attractions are not about gaming. *Jubilee!* (p145) is one of Vegas' long-running show-girl extravaganzas. After perform-ances, the leggy dancers often pose for their over-the-hill admirers at the casino's Indigo lounge. Or visitors can peek behind the cur-tains on a backstage tour (p146). From Las Vegas Blvd, a series of movable walkways underneath a garish neon canopy carry you inside. The monorail station is at the back, and an interior walkway connects to Paris Las Vegas.

BILL'S GAMBLIN' HALL & SALOON

☎ 737-2100; www.billslasvegas.com; 3595 Las Vegas Blvd S; Ⓜ Flamingo/ Caesars Palace

Lavish Tiffany-styled stained glass, stately chandeliers and polished dark wood dominate this pint-sized neo-Victorian casino. Only down-town's Main Street Station (p66) evokes turn-of-the-20th-century Nevada better. Opened as the Barbary Coast, this 1970s-era ca-sino claims 650 slot and video-poker machines and precious few table games. Downstairs, Drai's (p153) draws a hip post-clubbing crowd, while lounge acts like 'Big Elvis' play upstairs. Parking is almost impossible here; try walk-ing over from the monorail line instead.

CALIFORNIA

☎ 385-1222; www.thecal.com; 12 E Ogden Ave; 🚌 Deuce

At many Vegas casinos, a lucky spin of a slot machine will earn you a brand-spanking new BMW, a racy Jaguar or a red-hot convertible. At the downtown 'just-call-me-Cal' California, one very lucky nickel-slots player will someday ride home in – drum roll, please – a brand-new PT Cruiser! That simple fact tells you a lot about the 1970s-era Cal, 'the hotel with aloha spirit,' where even the dealers wear Ha-waiian shirts, because over 80% of

BEST LOW-ROLLER DIVES

Whether you're looking for 5¢ video-poker machines or roulette wheels with 25¢ minimum bets, bravely start slum-ming downtown at the **Golden Gate** (opposite), **Plaza** (p67) or **El Cortez** (opposite), or on the Strip at the loud-as-hell **Casino Royale** (opposite) or the **Stratosphere** (p60).

the Cal's guests hail from the 50th state. On the skybridge connecting to Main Street Station are photos of the Cal's Golden Arm Club, which immortalizes lucky shooters from the craps tables.

CASINO ROYALE

☎ 800-854-7666; www.casinoroyale hotel.com; 3411 Las Vegas Blvd S; M Harrah's/Imperial Palace

Tired of megaresort casinos stealing your dough courtesy of bad-odds video-poker machines and table games with ridiculous rules that inflate the house advantage (ie 'edge') beyond limits that even mobsters would find respectable? Well, the odds aren't great here either, but at least low-minimum wagers make it easier to stomach. The Casino Royale, a dingy downtown-style joint that somehow ended up on the Strip, squeezed between the Venetian and Harrah's, is a low-risk place for first-time gamblers, because almost no-one else knows what they're doing here either. Cheap drinks and fast food keep die-hard low rollers sated.

EL CORTEZ

☎ 385-5200; www.elcortezhotelcasino .com; 600 E Fremont St; Deuce

A classic dive dating back to 1940, El Cortez is choked with smoke but has vintage Vegas appeal in spades. In the crowded casino,

rough-edged local gamblers grudgingly allow accidental tourists like yourself to buy into the low-limit action on roulette, craps and other table games aimed at cheapskates and gambling novices. El Cortez is the kind of place where it's almost impossible to lose your shirt, but you'll need a few stiff drinks first. It's a few too many blocks east of the Fremont Street Experience. Then again, if that kind of thing bothered you, you wouldn't even be thinking about dropping by this seedy place.

GOLDEN GATE

☎ 385-1906; www.goldengatecasino .net; 1 E Fremont St; Deuce

This old-fashioned gambling hall and hotel has stood on the corner of Fremont and Main Sts since 1906, one year after this whistle-stop railway town was founded. The casino transformed into the Golden Gate in the 1950s, when a troupe of Italian-Americans from San Francisco decamped at what was once known as the 'Sal Sagev' (the city's name spelled backward, doncha know). Today the Golden Gate's hypnotic mechanical sign is almost as irresistible as its famous $1.99 shrimp cocktails (p118). The snug casino boasts lively craps tables and double-deck blackjack being dealt to the herky-jerky sounds of old-fashioned piano music.

CASINOS & GAMBLING

🅒 HARRAH'S

☎ 369-5000; www.harrahslasvegas
.com; 3475 Las Vegas Blvd S;
Ⓜ Harrah's/Imperial Palace

Though it's not nearly as rambunctious as Vegas' *carnaval* casino
hotel, the Rio (p58), Harrah's may
be the brightest, friendliest and
most playful casino on the Strip –
and it's swimming with gamblers.
An enormous backlit mural over
the hotel's front desk depicts the
greatest Las Vegas entertainers
of all time, and entertainment is
still the name of the game here,
with the Improv (p138) comedy
club and other headliner comics
and magicians. After dark, try out

for TJ's All-Star Karaoke (see the
boxed text, p139) at the piano
bar or get soused in the outdoor
Carnaval Court (p134), where flair
bartenders juggle fire.

🅒 IMPERIAL PALACE

☎ 731-3311; www.imperialpalace.com;
3535 Las Vegas Blvd S; Ⓜ Harrah's/
Imperial Palace

The blue-roofed pagoda facade and
faux–Far East theme are hokey, but
the zany atmosphere at what was
once the Flamingo Capri is quite
alright. The always-packed casino is
decked out in bamboo and rattan
under a dragon-motif ceiling. If you
liked the indie movie *The Cooler*,
you'll love it here. There are lots of
low-minimum table games to be
found here, but avoid the bad-odds
blackjack in the deceptively tempt-
ing Champagne Pit. Time your visit
to coincide with the evening shift
change of the 'dealertainers' (p78),
celebrity impersonators who do
double duty as dealers, or catch the
sham stars performing in Legends
in Concert (p146).

🅒 MAIN STREET STATION

☎ 387-1896; www.mainstreetcasino
.com; 200 N Main St; 🚌 Deuce

Throughout the filigreed neo-
Victorian casino are notable *objets
d'histoire*, most keeping to the
turn-of-the-19th-century theme.
Look out for an art-nouveau

Get into the spirit at Harrah's Carnaval Court (p134)

chandelier from Paris and stained-glass windows from silent-movie star Lillian Gish's mansion. Exquisite bronze chandeliers above the casino's central pit were originally installed in the 1890s Coca-Cola Building in Austin, Texas. Ornate mahogany woodwork now gracing the hotel registration desk and players' club was lifted out of a 19th-century Kentucky drugstore. Surprisingly, a graffiti-covered chunk of the Berlin Wall now supports the urinals in the men's restroom. Self-guided tour brochures are available at the hotel lobby desk, near the antique-filled Pullman Bar & Grille (p120).

MONTE CARLO
☎ 730-7777; www.montecarlo.com; 3770 Las Vegas Blvd S; 🚌 Deuce
Fronted by Corinthian colonnades, triumphal arches, petite dancing fountains and allegorical statuary, this not-so-elegant casino is still bustling and spacious. A magnificent marble-floored, crystal-chandeliered lobby with Palladian windows is reminiscent of a European grand hotel, but otherwise this is a poor person's Bellagio rather than an evocation of the grandeur of its namesake in Monaco. For entertainment, there's master magician Lance Burton (p138) and tacky, trashy Diablo's Cantina towering over the Strip out front.

ORLEANS
☎ 365-7111; www.orleanscasino.com; 4500 W Tropicana Ave; 🚌 free Strip shuttle
A mile west of the Strip, this N'awlins-themed casino hotel has done a so-so job of re-creating the Big Easy. Among its many diversions are the 70-lane bowling alley, 18-screen cineplex and specialty bars like Brendan's Irish Pub, which has live music some nights. Entertainment legends such as Willie Nelson and LeAnn Rimes have performed in the Orleans showroom, while megaconcerts and sports events take place in the arena (see the boxed text, p151). The high-ceilinged casino is an airy, rectangular room filled with thousands of ho-hum slot machines and table games.

PLAZA
☎ 386-2110; www.plazahotelcasino.com; 1 Main St; 🚌 Deuce
Built on the site of the old Union Pacific Railroad Depot, Jackie Gaughan's Plaza is a 1970s time capsule. Like most downtown joints, the down-at-heel Plaza is made for low-rollin' gamblers. Its tacky decor doesn't correspond to any known theme, unless the theme is cheap. And that's just fine with the Plaza's patrons, who are hypnotized by the penny slots, nickel video-poker machines and

$1 blackjack tables with sarcastic dealers. Feisty blue-haired ladies play for keeps upstairs in the 400-seat bingo room. Also upstairs is the Dome, a sports bar with cockpit views of the Fremont Street Experience.

🎰 RED ROCK CASINO RESORT SPA
☎ 797-7777; www.redrocklasvegas.com; 11011 W Charleston Blvd at I-215; 🚌 206

Poised within easy striking distance of the southwestern beauty of Red Rock Canyon (p160), this slick high-concept, high-design casino resort is built for suburbanites. It banks not only on its vast casino, but also on its adventure spa (p149) and above-average restaurants, such as the authentic Texas-style Salt Lick BBQ (p128).

🎰 RIVIERA
☎ 734-5110; www.rivierahotel.com; 2901 Las Vegas Blvd S; 🚌 Deuce

The Riviera was the first high-rise on the Strip when it opened in 1955. Liberace did the ribbon-cutting honors. Film auteur Orson Welles appeared on stage the next year performing – of all things – magic acts. A host of big-name entertainers have starred at the Riviera ever since, including Louis Armstrong, Duke Ellington and Tony Bennett. But that Hollywood glamour has been almost entirely lost by now. Inside the dimly lit, confusingly laid-out casino, Penny and Nickel Town are faves with the old-as-the-hills clientele, who love the hot, hot slot tournies. Outside the front entrance, a bawdy bronzed statue of the Riv's showgirls is fondly fondled by drunk tourists.

🎰 SAM'S TOWN
☎ 456-7777; www.samstownlv.com; 5111 Boulder Hwy at E Flamingo Rd & S Nellis Blvd; 🚌 107, 202

It's such a landmark on the local Vegas scene, the Killers named their sophomore album after it. Ranchers, cowboys and RVers flock here, and there's a helluva lot to keep 'em all amused. It's a rip-roarin' place to get your feet wet at table games, including some single-deck blackjack and electronic roulette. Or you can just peruse the country-and-western outfitter Sheplers (p89), go bowling and take in a flick at the cinema, or feed your inner glutton at Billy Bob's Steak House and Saloon, which dishes up a foot-long Grand Canyon chocolate layer cake.

🎰 SILVERTON
☎ 263-7777; www.silvertoncasino.com; 3333 Blue Diamond Rd, off I-15; 🚌 217

Built for the same redneck crowd as the Bass Pro Shops Outdoor

World (p96) next door, here you can keep plugging away nickels and quarters into all of those full-pay video-poker and slot machines, just like the RV-drivin' retirees who are camped at the RV park out back. Don't miss the coin-op miniature bowling inside an Airstream trailer at Hootie & the Blowfish's Shady Grove Lounge.

TROPICANA
☎ 739-2222; www.tropicanalv.com; 3801 Las Vegas Blvd S; M MGM Grand
Built in 1957, the Trop has had nearly half a century to sully its shine, lose its crowds and go the way of the Dunes and the Sands – ashes to ashes, dust to dust. But thanks to a few lifts and tucks, it just keeps hanging in there. There's still a festive, faux–Polynesian village feel to it all, with waterfall gardens and multi-level lagoon pools, although the tropical-paradise theme virtually disappears in the casino, except for some faded floral carpets. Entertaining options include the long-running Folies Bergère show-girl revue (p145) and yuk-yuks at the Comedy Stop (p138).

VEGAS CLUB
☎ 385-1664; www.vegasclubcasino.net; 18 E Fremont St; Deuce
A sports-themed casino hotel with a Hawaiian twist, the super-friendly Vegas Club is noteworthy for its collections of sports memorabilia, such as World Series autographed baseball bats. Naturally there's a race and sports book with bleacher seats inside the low-key casino, where dealers don baseball-style uniforms just like at a real stadium. Keep an eye out for the occasional full-pay video-poker machine or double-deck blackjack table.

How does a classic model take your fancy? Browse the wheels at Auto Collections (p95)

◉ SEE

Baby, there's no shortage of things to see in Las Vegas. In fact, the one sure bet in this gambling-hall town is that you absolutely won't have time to see or do it all. The city itself is inexhaustible (and that's the way we like it).

That goes double for the Strip, where the vast majority of casino hotels are standing and the array of free to stratospherically priced attractions can be head-spinning. You could spend all day and night in just one of the Strip's top megaresorts, and still not experience everything it offers.

When you grow weary of all that glitz on the Strip, it's worth checking out the vintage vibe on Fremont St downtown, the hipster scene in the 18b Arts District, offbeat museums and more in Las Vegas' outlying neighborhoods, or the Southwest's desert playgrounds outside the city limits (p155).

As you ambitiously sketch out your day over a brunch buffet, remember to factor in the substantial time it takes just to get around town.

CYBER MUSEUMS

Lots of memorabilia gets cast off in this ahistorical town. Thankfully, some of it ends up in the **UNLV Special Collections** (www.library.unlv.edu/speccol), where it's closely guarded by the university. The Lied Library holds a pit boss's ransom of books, photos, maps, posters, manuscripts and more from the city's early, hurly-burly days. The best way to visit is from the comfort of your own hotel room; online exhibits are free and available 24/7/365. UNLV's **Center for Gaming Research** (http://gaming.unlv.edu/v_museum) also hosts a virtual museum with such intriguing exhibits as the photographic survey of the Strip's glorious neon, a retrospective on the World Series of Poker, Rat Pack–era memorabilia and more.

Top left Tasty treats, downtown **Bottom left** Succumb to cliché and get hitched by Elvis in a Vegas wedding chapel (p84)

◉ ART GALLERIES & MUSEUMS

See also p78 for more unusual and outrageous museums.

◉ ARTS FACTORY

☎ 676-1111; www.theartsfactory.com; 101-109 E Charleston Blvd; ⏱ most galleries noon-5pm Tue-Sat, to 10pm on last Fri of each month; 🚌 108

Las Vegas' fractured art scene received an enormous boost in the late '90s when photographer Wes Isbutt accidentally founded this arts complex. Inside you'll find hit-and-miss, but always intriguing, local artists' workshops and galleries.

◉ ATOMIC TESTING MUSEUM

☎ 794-5161; www.atomictesting museum.org; 755 E Flamingo Rd; adult/concession $12/9; ⏱ 9am-5pm Mon-Sat, 1-5pm Sun; 🚌 202

Explore the modern history of atomic weapons in the Southwest USA desert at this top-notch multimedia museum. View historic footage inside the Ground Zero Theater, which mimics a concrete test bunker, after buying your tickets at the replica Nevada Test Site guard station. For more background on the museum, see p15.

◉ BELLAGIO GALLERY OF FINE ART

☎ 693-7871, 877-957-9777; www .bellagio.com; Bellagio, 3600 Las Vegas Blvd S; adult $15, concession $10-12; ⏱ 10am-6pm Sun-Thu, 10am-9pm Fri & Sat, last entry 30min before closing; Ⓜ Bally's/Paris

Since Steve Wynn sold his baby to MGM Mirage, the Bellagio hasn't been blessed with the same world-class art, but its petite fine-arts gallery still hosts blockbuster traveling shows. Original masterworks also hang inside the casino-hotel's Picasso (p103) restaurant.

Get up close at the Arts Factory

Maggie Smith
Manager and all-around guru at the Atomic Testing Museum (p15 & opposite)

What's the museum's mission? It's not just about science, but also human history. **How to find the 'Wow!' factor here** There's a lot of wonderful stuff to see, including surprisingly interactive exhibits. Step inside the Ground Zero Theater to watch historical footage of atomic testing during the Cold War era. **So, about atomic testing…was it a good or bad idea?** People need to make up their own minds. We present opinions from a lot of different angles, from scientists and people who actually worked at the Nevada Test Site to save-the-world political protestors. **Number-one reason why everyone should visit** It's not just about Nevada, but also US and world history, and it's a topic that's still relevant today. **Where else can tourists go to learn about Las Vegas' hard-to-find history?** The Clark County Museum (p76), which has walk-through historical houses on its 'Heritage St.'

CLARK COUNTY MUSEUM

☎ 455-7955; www.accessclarkcounty .com; 1830 S Boulder Hwy, Henderson; adult/concession $1.50/1; ⏰ 9am-4:30pm; 🚌 402; ♿

On the valley outskirts, this humble but jam-packed museum merits a stop en route to Hoover Dam. Inside you'll find exhibits on the history of Las Vegas as an ancient sea, Native American camp and Western frontier town. Step outside the museum onto Heritage St and walk through beautifully restored historic houses.

COMMERCE STREET STUDIOS

☎ 678-6278; www.commercestreet studios.com; 1551 S Commerce St; ⏰ hours vary; 🚌 108

In downtown's 18b Arts District, these eclectic and independent artists' studios are ground zero for all of the First Friday (p14) hoopla.

LAS VEGAS ART MUSEUM

☎ 360-8000; www.lasvegasartmuseum .org; 9600 W Sahara Ave, west of S Fort Apache Rd; adult $6, concession $3-5; ⏰ 10am-5pm Tue-Sat, 1-5pm Sun, guided tours 2pm Sat & Sun; 🚌 204

Contemporary art shines in this small, white edifice filled with light and cutting-edge exhibitions from across the country and abroad. A Smithsonian affiliate, it focuses on the art of the Southwest. The gift shop sells original, affordable works by Nevada artisans and craftspeople.

NEON MUSEUM

☎ 387-6366; www.neonmuseum.org; ⏰ Fremont St galleries 24hr, boneyard tours by reservation only; 🚌 Deuce (Fremont St), 113 (boneyard)

Plaques tell the story of each sign in this alfresco assemblage of vintage neon. Genie lamps, glowing martini glasses and 1940s motel marquees brighten up downtown, especially inside the Neonopolis and on cul-de-sacs north of the Fremont Street Experience (p80). Tours of the giant 'boneyard' of rescued signs are by appointment only. The permanent museum is still a work-in-progress.

SPRINGS PRESERVE

☎ 822-7700; www.springspreserve.org; 333 S Valley View Blvd; adult $19, concession $11-17; ⏰ 10am-6pm; 🚌 104; ♿

A major 'green' achievement for the city, this fascinating museum complex (also see p24) weaves together the natural and cultural history of Las Vegas in the OriGen Experience museum, and examines a more sustainable future in the Desert Living Center. Walk the desert gardens and interpretive trails, sup at chef Wolfgang Puck's eco-café and pick up wildflower seeds in the gift shop.

UNLV MARJORIE BARRICK MUSEUM

☎ 895-3381; http://hrcweb.nevada.edu/museum; 4505 S Maryland Parkway; admission free; 🕒 8am-4:45pm Mon-Fri, 10am-2pm Sat; 🚌 109; 👤

Learn about Las Vegas' original inhabitants – the southern Paiutes – and other Native American tribes from around the Southwest, along with pre-Columbian American artifacts. Show up at noon every other Friday for an interactive feeding experience with the museum's resident reptiles. Outside is a small xeriscaped demonstration garden of Mojave Desert plants.

🔵 GARDENS & WILDLIFE

The trails and gardens at the eco-conscious Springs Preserve (opposite and p24) are open daily by donation.

🔵 BELLAGIO CONSERVATORY & BOTANICAL GARDEN

☎ 693-7111; www.bellagio.com; Bellagio, 3600 Las Vegas Blvd S; 🕒 24hr; Ⓜ Bally's/Paris

Beyond the hotel lobby, itself adorned with Dale Chihuly's sculpture of 2000 vibrant hand-blown glass flowers, the Bellagio's conservatory houses ostentatious floral arrangements that are bizarrely installed by crane through a soaring 50ft-high ceiling. The effect is ridiculously unnatural, but that doesn't stop crowds from gathering.

🔵 FLAMINGO WILDLIFE HABITAT

☎ 733-3111; www.flamingolasvegas.com; Flamingo, 3555 Las Vegas Blvd S; 🕒 24hr; Ⓜ Flamingo/Caesars Palace

Escape from the casino madness into a dozen acres of gardens, pools, waterfalls and waterways that are filled with swans, exotic birds and ornamental koi (carp). Chilean flamingos and African penguins wander around, and palm trees and jungle plants flourish in the midst of the desert.

🔵 LION HABITAT AT MGM GRAND

☎ 891-7777; www.mgmgrand.com; MGM Grand, 3799 Las Vegas Blvd S; 🕒 11am-10pm; Ⓜ MGM Grand

MGM owns many of the magnificent felines, all descendants of the movie company's original mascot, but only two are shown off in this multimillion-dollar enclosure at any given time. The big cats sprawl atop a walk-through tunnel, separated from your head by only a sheet of protective glass and a few feet of air. The animals do look rudely confined, though.

LAS VEGAS

SEE

MIRAGE CASINO HOTEL
☎ 791-7111; www.mirage.com; Mirage, 3400 Las Vegas Blvd S; ⏱ 24hr; 🚌 Harrah's/Imperial Palace

This high-roller casino is replete with a rainforest atrium under a 100ft-tall conservatory dome filled with jungle foliage, meandering streams and soothing cascades. Woven into the waterscape are scores of bromeliads fed by a computerized misting system. Exotic scents waft through the hotel lobby, where a 20,000-gallon saltwater aquarium harbors 60 species of tropical critters, from puffer fish to pygmy sharks.

SHARK REEF
☎ 632-4555; www.mandalaybay .com; Mandalay Bay, 3950 Las Vegas Blvd S; adult/concession incl audioguide $16/11; ⏱ 10am-11pm, last entry 10pm; 🚌 Deuce

M-Bay's unusual walk-through aquarium is home to 2000 submarine beasties, including jellyfish, moray eels, stingrays and, yes, some sharks. Other rare and endangered toothy reptiles on display include some of the world's last remaining golden crocodiles. A staff of biologists, scuba-diver caretakers and naturalists are available to chat as you wander around. Better yet, take the behind-the-scenes tour ($8).

SIEGFRIED & ROY'S SECRET GARDEN & DOLPHIN HABITAT
☎ 791-7188; www.miragehabitat .com; Mirage, 3400 Las Vegas Blvd S; adult/concession incl audioguide $15/10; ⏱ 11am-5:30pm Mon-Fri, 10am-5:30pm Sat & Sun, 10am-7pm daily in summer, last entry 30min before closing; 🚌 Deuce

All of the feats of conservation bragged about on the free audio tour can't compensate for enclosures built much too small for animals such as snow leopards, black jaguars and white lions and tigers, who roam the world's wildest places. The claustrophobic Atlantic bottlenose dolphin pools may also make animal lovers sick at heart.

QUIRKY LAS VEGAS

IMPERIAL PALACE DEALERTAINERS
☎ 731-3311; www.imperialpalace.com; Imperial Palace, 3535 Las Vegas Blvd S; ⏱ shows every 30min noon-4am; 🚌 Harrah's/Imperial Palace

Award-winning celebrity impersonators (p146) do double-duty as 'dealertainers,' jumping up from the blackjack tables and champagne pit to show off their song-and-dance skills on stage. Show up for the shift change at 8pm. Don't worry: Elvis never, ever leaves the building.

STRIPPER 101

Exotic dancers are Vegas icons. But sexy pole dancing as your new exercise routine? Marketed as 'pole dancing for housewives,' exotic-dancing classes are offered in Vegas to help bring out your inner blonde bombshell. The original experience, **Stripper 101** (☎ 260-7200; www .stripper101.com; Planet Hollywood, 3667 Las Vegas Blvd S; tickets from $40; ⏰ schedule varies; Ⓜ Bally's/Paris), is in a cabaret setting complete with strobe lights, cocktails and feather boas. It's popular with bachelorettes, who graduate with a certificate guaranteeing they're a 'genuine Las Vegas stripper.' No nudity is allowed, so bring comfy workout clothes and shoes, plus a pair of high heels to practice strutting your stuff in.

Ⓒ LIBERACE MUSEUM

☎ 798-5595; www.liberace.org; 1775 E Tropicana Ave; adult/concession $15/10; ⏰ 10am-5pm Tue-Sat, noon-4pm Sun, guided tours 11am Tue-Sat & 2pm Tue-Sun; 🚌 201

For connoisseurs of kitschy celebrity shrines, this memorial to 'Mr Showmanship' houses the most flamboyant art cars, outrageously cheesy costumes and ornate pianos you'll ever see. There's a hand-painted Pleyel, on which Chopin played; a Rolls-Royce covered in mirrored tiles; and a wardrobe exhibit full of feathered capes and million-dollar furs.

Ⓒ MADAME TUSSAUDS LAS VEGAS

☎ 862-7800; www.madametussauds .com; outside Venetian, 3377 Las Vegas Blvd S; adult $24, concession $14-18; ⏰ 10am-9pm Sun-Thu, 10am-10pm Fri & Sat; Ⓜ Harrah's/Imperial Palace

By the Venetian's moving Rialto Bridge walkway is this unique interactive wax museum, where you can strike a pose with Elvis, play golf with Tiger Woods, sing like you're on *American Idol* or put on Playboy bunny ears and sit on Hugh Hefner's lap (be sure to touch him, because Hef's made of silicone – how apropos!).

Ⓒ PINBALL HALL OF FAME

www.pinballmuseum.org; 3330 E Tropicana Ave at S Pecos Rd; admission free, most games 25-50¢; ⏰ 11am-11pm Sun-Thu, 11am-midnight Fri & Sat; 🚌 201

Tim Arnold lets anyone play his 200-plus collection of vintage pinball, video-arcade and carnival-sideshow games, all dating from the 1950s to the '90s. Take time to read the handwritten cards, which describe the priceless collection. Profits from every quarter you drop into the slots go to charity. The Pinball Hall of Fame is next to a discount cinema far east of the Strip.

LAS VEGAS

SEE

SLOTS A' FUN
☎ 734-0410; 2890 Las Vegas Blvd S;
🕐 24hr; 🚌 Deuce

For cheap booze and cheap thrills, it's tough to beat this low-brow dive. Grab a coupon book, give the giant slot machine a free spin and scarf down a few 75¢ beers and $1 half-pound hot dogs. Then kick back, relax and enjoy the laughable lounge acts. Park at Circus Circus (p44) next door.

👁 SHOWY SPECTACULARS

On the Strip, many casinos compete to dream up the biggest, best free shows. Downtown, nothing beats the cheesy Fremont Street Experience.

CIRCUS CIRCUS MIDWAY
☎ 734-0410; www.circuscircus.com; Circus Circus, 2880 Las Vegas Blvd S; 🕐 shows every 30min 11am-midnight; 🚌 Deuce

Free circus acts – trapeze artists, high-wire workers, jugglers and unicyclists – steal center stage directly above this Austin Powers–era casino's main floor. Over in the peanut gallery, grab a free seat at the revolving Horse-A-Round Bar, made famous by Hunter S Thompson's gonzo-journalism epic *Fear and Loathing in Las Vegas*.

FOUNTAINS OF BELLAGIO
☎ 693-7111; www.bellagio.com; Bellagio, 3600 Las Vegas Blvd S; 🕐 shows every 30min 3-8pm Mon-Fri, noon-8pm Sat & Sun, every 15min 8pm-midnight daily; Ⓜ Bally's/Paris

With a backdrop of Tuscan architecture, the Bellagio's faux Lake Como and dancing fountains are the antithesis of the desert – and a mighty waster of precious well water, too. The fountain show's recorded soundtrack varies, so cross your fingers that it will be Italian opera or ol' Blue Eyes crooning 'Luck Be a Lady,' instead of country-western twang.

FREMONT STREET EXPERIENCE
☎ 678-5600; www.vegasexperience.com; Fremont St, btwn Main St & Las Vegas Blvd; 🕐 shows hourly dusk-midnight; 🚌 Deuce

The 1400ft-long canopy over downtown's Fremont St is steroid-enhanced by 550,000 watts of concert-hall sound and a super-big Viva Vision screen. When the 12.5-million synchronized LEDs come on, cheesy sound-and-light shows are awesome enough to hypnotize every spectator (especially drunks). A misting system built into the canopy spritzes cool relief on steamy, hot summer days.

WELCOME TO FABULOUS LAS VEGAS

Straddling Las Vegas Blvd, south of the Strip, is the city's most iconic sign, 'Welcome to Fabulous Las Vegas Nevada.' Cruising by, you might see limos illegally parked alongside the road and camera-happy tourists dashing out onto the median to get a souvenir photo of themselves by the vintage sign.

Of course, when Betty Willis designed it in 1959 with an atomic-modern starburst at the top, it wasn't fabulously retro – it was cutting-edge hip. If you miss out on a real-live photo op, you can order a mini working model of the sign (it lights up! it flashes!) online at www.lvsignco.com.

MIRAGE VOLCANO

☎ 791-7111; www.mirage.com; Mirage, 3400 Las Vegas Blvd S; ⏰ shows hourly 8pm-midnight, starting 6pm/7pm in winter/spring; 🚌 Deuce

When the Mirage's trademark artificial volcano erupts out of a three-acre lagoon with a roar, it inevitably brings traffic on the Strip to a screeching halt. Be on the lookout for wisps of smoke escaping from the top that signal the fiery Polynesian-style inferno is about to begin.

SIRENS OF TI

☎ 894-7111; www.treasureisland.com; TI (Treasure Island), 3300 Las Vegas Blvd S; ⏰ shows usually 7pm, 8:30pm, 10pm & 11pm, weather permitting; 🚌 Deuce

The laughably spicy Sirens of TI show is a hilarious mock sea battle of the sexes that pits sultry femme-fatale pirates dressed like lingerie models against manly renegade freebooters.

With a booming soundtrack and pyrotechnics, the show's ships – a Spanish privateer vessel and a British frigate – face off in the cove outside the casino.

THRILL RIDES & AMUSEMENTS

ADVENTUREDOME

☎ 794-3939; www.circuscircus.com; Circus Circus, 2880 Las Vegas Blvd S; per ride $4-7, day pass adult/concession $25/15; ⏰ 10am-midnight in summer, off-season hours vary; 🚌 Deuce

Enclosed by over 8000 pink-glass panes, Circus Circus' indoor amusement park is packed with thrills. Must-rides include the double-loop, double-corkscrew Canyon Blaster and the Sling Shot tower ride that packs a whopping four Gs of acceleration. Older kids get a rock-climbing wall, bungee-jumping area, mini golf and 4D special-effect 'ridefilms.' Clowns perform free shows throughout the day.

CONEY ISLAND EMPORIUM & ROLLER COASTER

☎ 740-6969; www.nynyhotelcasino.com; New York–New York, 3790 Las Vegas Blvd S; roller coaster $14 (re-ride $7), games from 50¢; ◷ 11am-11pm Sun-Thu, 10:30am-midnight Fri & Sat; Ⓜ MGM Grand

Though your head and shoulders will take a beating, the coaster's heartline twist-and-dive maneuver produces a sensation similar to that felt by a pilot during a barrel roll in a fighter plane. The rest of the four-minute ride includes stomach-dropping dipsy-dos, high-banked turns, a 540-degree spiral and blink-and-you'll-miss-it Strip views. Enter through the Coney Island Emporium video-game arcade (with bumper cars!).

EIFFEL TOWER EXPERIENCE

☎ 946-7000; www.parislasvegas.com; Paris Las Vegas, 3655 Las Vegas Blvd S; adult/concession $10/7; ◷ 9:30am-12:30am, weather permitting; Ⓜ Bally's/Paris

How authentic is the half-scale tower? Gustave Eiffel's original drawings were consulted, but the 50-story ersatz replica is welded rather than riveted together. It's also fireproof and engineered to withstand a major earthquake. Ascend in a glass elevator to the observation deck for panoramic

No French required at the Eiffel Tower Experience

views over the Strip, the Las Vegas Valley and the rugged desert mountains.

ESPN ZONE SPORTS ARENA

☎ 933-3776; http://espnzone.com; New York–New York, 3790 Las Vegas Blvd S; ◷ 11am-10:30pm Sun-Thu, 11am-11:30pm Fri & Sat; Ⓜ MGM Grand

Head upstairs from the sports-themed bar and eatery to play state-of-the-art boxing, pro golfing, skiing and other virtual-reality arcade games. You can also go duckpin bowling or scramble up a 30ft rock-climbing wall.

🎮 GAMEWORKS

☎ 432-4263; www.gameworks.com; Showcase Mall, 3785 Las Vegas Blvd S; games 30¢-$3.50, 1hr/2hr/3hr/all-day unlimited play $20/25/30/35; 🕐 10am-midnight Sun-Thu, 10am-1am Fri & Sat; Ⓜ MGM Grand

Conceived by Steven Spielberg and developed by DreamWorks SKG with Sega and Universal Studios, this high-tech arcade inhabits a large underground space with a full bar, 75ft-high climbing wall, pool tables and loads of multiplayer virtual-reality games (bring lots of buddies). It's only ever crowded – not to mention fun – after 9pm, when no unaccompanied minors are allowed.

🎮 POLE POSITION RACEWAY

☎ 227-7223; www.racep2r.com; 4175 S Arville St; race per adult/junior $25/22; 🕐 11am-midnight; 🚌 free Strip shuttle

Dreamed up by Nascar and Supercross racing champs, this European-style raceway modeled on Formula One road courses boasts the fastest indoor go-karts in the USA, exciting whether you're a teen novice or a full-grown adult speed freak. Drivers must be 48in/56in tall to join the junior/adult kart races.

🎮 RICHARD PETTY DRIVING EXPERIENCE

☎ 644-4443, 800-237-3889; www.1800bepetty.com; Las Vegas Motor Speedway, 6975 Speedway Blvd, off I-15; 🕐 call for schedule

Curious about what it's like to be in high-speed pursuit? Here's your chance to ride shotgun during a Nascar-style qualifying run ($149) or drive yourself ($399) in a 600-horsepower stock car reaching speeds of over 150mph. Also at the Speedway (p151), the **Mario Andretti Racing School** (☎ 877-722-3527; http://andrettiracing.com) offers cheaper ride-along and race opportunities.

🎮 SPEED & LAS VEGAS CYBER SPEEDWAY

☎ 737-2111; www.saharavegas.com; Sahara, 2535 Las Vegas Blvd S; single ride/all-day pass $10/20; 🕐 Speed 2-10pm Thu-Mon, extended summer & holiday hours, Cyber Speedway from 11am daily; Ⓜ Sahara

The Speedway's Indy car simulators are so lifelike that they excite real Formula One drivers. The artificial racers are bolted to hydraulic platforms fronting wraparound screens that are adrenaline-pumping in their realism. Speed, an electromagnetic roller coaster, slingshots to a top speed of 70mph as it zooms through the Sahara's signature marquee.

STRATOSPHERE TOWER
☎ 380-7777; www.stratospherehotel
.com; Stratosphere, 2000 Las Vegas Blvd
S; adult/concession elevator $14/10,
incl 3 thrill rides $28, all-day pass $34;
⏱ 10am-1am Sun-Thu, 10am-2am Fri &
Sat, weather permitting; Ⓜ Sahara
The world's highest thrill rides
await, a whopping 110 stories
above the Strip. Big Shot straps
riders into completely exposed
seats that zip up the tower's pinnacle, while Insanity spins riders
out over the tower's edge. Views
from xScream are good, but the
ride itself is a dud – save your
dough for the lounge at Romance
at Top of the World (p137).

VENETIAN GONDOLAS
☎ 414-4300; www.venetian.com;
Venetian, 3355 Las Vegas Blvd S;
indoor/outdoor ride per person $15/12.50,
private 2-passenger ride $60/50;
⏱ ticket booth opens at 9am/10am for
indoor/outdoor rides, departures 10am-
10:45pm Sun-Thu, 10am-11:45pm Fri &
Sat; Ⓜ Harrah's/Imperial Palace
Graceful bridges, flowing canals,
vibrant piazzas and stone walkways almost capture the romantic
spirit of Venice inside the Grand
Canal Shoppes (p93), especially
when viewed from the seat of a
floating gondola. Rides are short
(under 15 minutes), but sweet.
Same-day, in-person reservations
required.

WEDDING CHAPELS
Before you get hitched, you'll need
a marriage license (see p168).

A SPECIAL MEMORY
WEDDING CHAPEL
☎ 384-2211, 800-962-7798; www
.aspecialmemory.com; 800 S 4th St;
⏱ 8am-10pm Sun-Thu, 8am-midnight
Fri & Sat; 🚌 Deuce
The drive-up window on Lovers
Lane has a wedding menu board
(breakfast packages cost from $55,
plus don't forget to tip the minister). A limo ride or an appearance
by Elvis, Cher or Grandpa Munster
are priced à la carte.

GRACELAND WEDDING
CHAPEL
☎ 382-0091, 800-824-5732; www
.gracelandchapel.com; 619 Las Vegas
Blvd S; ⏱ 9am-11pm; 🚌 Deuce
Offering the original Elvis impersonator wedding (from $199) for
over 50 years. If it's good enough
for rock stars, then it's probably
good enough for you, too.

LITTLE CHURCH OF
THE WEST
☎ 739-7971, 800-821-2452; www
.littlechurchlv.com; 4617 Las Vegas Blvd S;
⏱ 8am-midnight; 🚌 Deuce
Beginners' wedding packages cost
just $199 at this quiet, quaint little
wooden chapel built in 1942, in

the shadow of the South Strip, as seen in the classic Elvis movie *Viva Las Vegas*. Spanish- and French-speaking ministers are available (by reservation only).

📷 MAVERICK HELICOPTERS
☎ 261-0007, 888-261-4414; www.maverickhelicopter.com; 🕐 by reservation only

Take a flight with Grand Canyon (p156) or Valley of Fire (p158) wedding packages (from $699), including videography, flowers for the bride and groom, a champagne toast and wedding cake upon landing. Up to three guests fly free.

📷 VEGAS WEDDING CHAPEL
☎ 933-3464, 800-823-4095; www.702wedding.com; 555 S 3rd St; 🕐 8am-midnight; 🚌 105

Here you've got the only walk-up wedding window in the world, plus a cathedral-esque chapel, sunset terrace and gardens. Weddings can also be arranged at scenic outdoor spots in the desert and mountains, as well as at the Grand Canyon.

📷 VIVA LAS VEGAS WEDDINGS
☎ 384-0771, 800-574-4450; www.viva lasvegasweddings.com; 1205 Las Vegas Blvd S; 🕐 office 9am-5pm, ceremony reservations 11am-9pm; 🚌 Deuce

Wacky themed wedding ceremonies (imagine vampires, Harley hogs or Cirque du Soleil–esque aerial acrobats), which can be broadcast online, are as kitschy as all get-out. More traditional wedding packages cost from $199.

📷 WEE KIRK O' THE HEATHER
☎ 382-9830, 800-843-5266; www .weekirk.com; 231 Las Vegas Blvd S; 🕐 10am-8pm; 🚌 Deuce

The oldest continuously operating wedding chapel in Las Vegas (since 1940), and it's conveniently close to the county marriage bureau. Wedding packages booked online cost from just $50.

🛍 SHOP

Surprisingly, Las Vegas has evolved into a so-phisticated shopping destination. International haute-couture purveyors on the Strip cater to cashed-up clientele, whether it's catwalk fashions fresh off this year's runways, diamond jewels once worn by royalty or imported sports cars. But Sin City is still the kind of place where porn star–worthy bling, Elvis wigs and other tacky trash just flies off the shelves, too.

If all you want is a T-shirt, bumper sticker or shot glass announcing that you've finally been to 'Fabulous Las Vegas,' tacky souvenirs are everywhere. But if you're looking for something more unusual, the city's specialty shops are full of cool kitsch and priceless collectibles, from vintage casino memorabilia to showgirls' feather boas and real-life poker tables.

Retail shopping hours are normally 10am to 9pm (to 6pm Sunday), but casino shops, arcades and malls typically stay open until 11pm (midnight on Friday and Saturday). Christmas is one of the few holidays when most shops close.

SHOPPING AREAS

Mega-malls dominate the scene. The Strip has the highest-octane shopping action, with upscale boutiques found inside casino resorts from the Palazzo south to Mandalay Place. Downtown and west of the Strip are where to cruise for wigs, naughty adult goods and trashy lingerie. Vintage clothing stores, antiques shops and art galleries are reviving the Naked City, radiating outward from the intersection of Main St and Charleston Blvd. East of the Strip near UNLV, Maryland Parkway is chock-a-block with hip, cheapo shops. Trendy one-off boutiques are scarce, but they're popping up in the 'burbs, where discount outlet malls are found.

Top left For winning tips, visit Gamblers Book Shop (p90) **Bottom left** Glam it up at Rainbow Feather Dyeing Co (p99)

CLOTHING & JEWELRY

THE ATTIC
☎ 388-4088; www.theatticlasvegas
.com; 1018 S Main St; ⊙ 10am-5pm
Mon-Thu, 10am-6pm Fri, 11am-6pm Sat;
🚌 108

A $1 'lifetime pass' (applied to your
first purchase) is required to enter
this fantastic vintage emporium,
but it's worth it, even if you don't
buy anything. Be mesmerized by
fabulous hats, outrageous wigs,
hippie-chic clubwear and lounge-
lizard furnishings. An upstairs

coffee bar dishes up freshly made
soups, salads and sandwiches.

BUFFALO EXCHANGE
☎ 791-3960; www.buffaloexchange
.com; 4110 S Maryland Parkway;
⊙ 10am-8pm Mon-Sat, 11am-7pm Sun;
🚌 109, 202

Trade in your nearly new garb
for cash or credit at this savvy
second-hand chain. Don't worry:
it has combed through the dingy
thrift-store stuff and culled only
the best 1940s to '80s vintage,
clubwear, costuming goodies and
designer duds.

Get the vintage vibe at The Attic

⬚ EPIC SHOOS

☎ 388-4343; www.epicshoos.com; 1209 S Main St; ☽ noon-7pm Mon-Sat; 🚌 108

In the offbeat downtown arts district, this minimalist sneaker boutique stays under the radar, but still carries the hippest kicks in uber-cool collectible styles for outfitting urban legends in the making.

⬚ FRED LEIGHTON

☎ 693-7050; Via Bellagio, 3600 Las Vegas Blvd S; ☽ 10am-midnight; Ⓜ Bally's/Paris

Many of Hollywood's red-carpet adornments are on loan from the world's most prestigious collection of antique jewelry, notably art deco and art nouveau. In Las Vegas, unlike at the uptight NYC outlet, they'll let almost anyone try on finery that once belonged to royalty. Price tags for pieces easily top $1 million at this veritable museum of jewels.

⬚ SHEPLERS

☎ 454-5266; www.sheplers.com; Sam's Town, 5111 Boulder Hwy; ☽ 10am-10pm; 🚌 107, 202

In business since 1899, this reliable Western outfitter has everything you'll need to dress up like a real cowboy or cowgirl: blue jeans, button-down shirts, leather jackets, felt fur hats and even embroidered ostrich-skin boots.

⬚ VALENTINO'S ZOOTSUIT CONNECTION

☎ 383-9555; www.valentinoszootsuit connection.com; 906 S 6th St; ☽ 11am-5pm Mon-Sat; 🚌 Deuce

Lots of timeless outfits get cast off in this ahistorical town. Some end up at this upscale resale boutique, which specializes in men's and women's clothing from the turn of the 20th century right through to the 1970s. A sweet (and stylish!) husband-and-wife team outfits party-goers with custom swinging zootsuits, cocktail dresses, Old Hollywood glamour gowns, fringed Western wear and felt fedoras.

⬚ WILLIAMS COSTUME COMPANY

☎ 384-1384; 1226 S 3rd St; ☽ 10am-5:15pm Mon-Sat; 🚌 105

Williams Costume Company has supplied the Strip's starlets with do-it-yourself costuming goods since 1957. Check out the headshots in the dressing rooms, then go pick up some rhinestones, sequins, feathers etc – you go, girl. Costume rentals are also available.

⬚ ZAPPOS.COM SHOE OUTLET

☎ 943-7900; www.zappos.com; 7770 S Dean Martin Dr; ☽ 9am-9pm; 🚌 free Strip shuttle

A specialty online shoe retailer stocks crazy brand-names at serious discounts here, with pairs for women and men available up to size 16. Try on *Sex and the City*–style pumps, sporty kicks, big boots and kitten heels. Bejeweled bags and belts make any outfit a knockout. Call for free Strip shuttle schedules.

MUSIC & BOOKS

For riveting reads about Las Vegas, see p185.

ALTERNATE REALITY COMICS

☎ 736-3673; www.alternatereality comics.net; 4800 S Maryland Parkway; noon-6pm Sun-Tue, 11am-7pm Wed-Sat; 🚌 109

In the same UNLV strip mall as a tattoo parlor and an underground vinyl shop, this unbelievably cool comic shop for adults fills its shelves with the hippest graphic novels, Japanese manga, indie 'zines and collectibles for connoisseurs.

BAUMAN RARE BOOKS

☎ 948-1617; www.baumanrarebooks .com; Shoppes at Palazzo, Palazzo, 3327 Las Vegas Blvd S; 10am-11pm Sun-Thu, 10am-midnight Fri & Sat; Ⓜ Harrah's/Imperial Palace

Hidden inside the Palazzo, enter a bibliophile's paradise, where rare and first editions of the *Wizard of Oz* and Truman Capote's *In Cold Blood* stand on giant-sized shelves. Lavishly illustrated antiquarian titles lie under glass display cases. Staff may raise their eyebrows at casual browsers, who may *not* touch the tomes.

GAMBLERS BOOK SHOP

☎ 382-7555, 800-522-1777; www .gamblersbook.com; 630 S 11th St; 9am-5pm Mon-Sat; 🚌 109, 206

This off-the-beaten-path gem stocks just about every book ever written about gaming strategy and Las Vegas, including out-of-print titles. The clientele, some of whom look as if they might have been around since the Rat Pack era, can dispense valuable edge-beating advice.

ZIA RECORDS

☎ 735-4942; www.ziarecords.com; 4225 S Eastern Ave; 10am-midnight; 🚌 110, 202

Calling itself the 'last real record store,' this Arizona-based vendor has a warehouse full of ear-tickling sounds, including a locals-only section where you just might dig up a demo by the next breakout Vegas band. Live in-store performances happen on a stage with the warning sign: 'No moshing allowed.'

NAUGHTY NOVELTIES

There are full-service lingerie shops inside many strip clubs (p152). All those hard-working beefy guys and sultry women obviously don't have time to make their own G-strings and tasseled undies!

A SLIGHTLY SINFUL ADVENTURE

☎ 387-1006; 1232 Las Vegas Blvd S; ⏱ 10am-10pm Sun-Thu, 10am-midnight Fri & Sat; 🚌 Deuce

For voyeurs, admiring the trashy stripper-worthy apparel and X-rated toys in the presence of the, ahem, working-girl clientele out front can make a visit worth the effort.

ADULT SUPERSTORE

☎ 798-0144; 3850 W Tropicana Ave; ⏱ 24hr; 🚌 201

This enormous, well-lit porn warehouse is a sexual fantasyland of toys, books, porn magazines and movies, 'marital enhancement products' and titillating accessories. Solo guys gravitate toward the XXX arcade upstairs.

BARE ESSENTIALS

☎ 247-4711; www.bareessentialsvegas.com; 4029 W Sahara Ave; ⏱ 10am-7pm Mon-Sat, noon-5pm Sun; 🚌 204

Pros swear by BE for business attire. It's heavy on theme wear – lots of cheerleader and schoolgirl outfits. Next door, **Bad Attitude Boutique** (☎ 646-9669; www.badattitude.com; ⏱ 11am-7pm Mon-Fri, noon-6pm Sat, noon-5pm Sun) makes custom-made corsets and bustiers, goth fetish wear and burlesque fashions, while

BEST UNIQUE BOUTIQUES

> Talulah G (Fashion Show, p92; Boca Park Fashion Village, p92)
> Stash (Miracle Mile Shops, p94)
> Annie Creamcheese (Shoppes at Palazzo, p94)
> Bettie Page (Miracle Mile Shops, p94)
> Love Jones (Hard Rock, p93)

neighboring **Red Shoes** (☎ 889-4442; ⏱ 10:30am-8pm Mon-Sat, noon-6:30pm Sun) stocks knee-high boots, stripper stilettos and glittery platforms.

DÉJÀ VU LOVE BOUTIQUE

☎ 731-5652; 3275 Industrial Rd; ⏱ 10am-4am; 🚌 116

Sidling up next to a strip club, this candy-colored sex shop stays open until the wee hours. Drop in for a pick-me-up, maybe passionfruit-flavored lube, a bouncy paddle or a very adult DVD to enjoy in your hotel room. Bachelor/bachelorette parties welcome.

PARADISE ELECTRO STIMULATIONS

☎ 474-2991, 800-339-6953; www.peselectro.com; 1509 W Oakey Blvd; ⏱ 10am-6pm Mon-Thu, 10am-7pm Fri, noon-6pm Sat; 🚌 105

'Innovating human sexuality since 1986,' this dungeon-esque

fetish boutique is tucked away on the wrong side of the tracks. It's the exotic, neon-lit home of owner Dante Amore's legendary auto-erotic chair, which must be seen (and felt) to be believed. Yeeowch.

STRINGS OF LAS VEGAS
☎ 873-7820; 4970 Arville St; ⏲ noon-8pm Mon-Sat, 1-7pm Sun; 🚌 104, 201
It's no surprise to see a Hummer limo parked outside this industrial strip-mall warehouse of adult and fetish fashions. Watch go-go and exotic dancers get dressed (or undressed, rather) from head to toe here, with jewelry, platform shoes and the shortest skirts and scantiest G-strings you've ever seen. Custom-made designs available.

SHOPPING MALLS & ARCADES

BOCA PARK FASHION VILLAGE
740-750 S Rampart Blvd, north of Charleston Blvd; ⏲ 11am-7pm Mon-Sat, 11am-6pm Sun; 🚌 206
Racking up the hottest, hard-to-find designer labels, many of Vegas' independent clothing boutiques have gravitated toward the moneyed suburb of Summerlin. Fashionistas favor **C Level** (☎ 933-6867), **Talulah G** (☎ 932-7000), **Pink** (☎ 932-7465) and sweatshop-free LA import **American Apparel** (☎ 851-7474).

THE DISTRICT
☎ 564-8595, 877-564-8595; www.the districtatgvr.com; Green Valley Ranch, 2240 Village Walk Dr, Henderson, off I-215 exit Green Valley Parkway; ⏲ 10am-9pm Mon-Sat, 11am-7pm Sun; 🚌 111
An off-Strip shopping magnet, the open-air upmarket District has a cool mix of four-dozen shops, such as REI, the West Coast outdoor sports retailer. A free trolley shuttles over to 'The Green,' where Pink designer boutique sets up shop.

FASHION SHOW
☎ 784-7000; www.thefashionshow .com; 3200 Las Vegas Blvd S; ⏲ 10am-9pm Mon-Sat, 11am-7pm Sun; 🚌 Deuce
Size *does* matter. Though unique shops are sparse at Nevada's biggest and flashiest mall, there are 250-plus chain storefronts, all anchored by giant department stores. Movie stars drop by Talulah G boutique. It's all topped off by 'The Cloud,' a multimedia canopy that resembles a flamenco hat.

FORUM SHOPS
☎ 893-4800; www.simon.com; Caesars Palace, 3500 Las Vegas Blvd S; ⏲ 10am-11pm Sun-Thu, 11am-midnight Fri & Sat; Ⓜ Flamingo/Caesars Palace
Franklins fly out of Fendi bags faster here than in the high-roller casinos. Caesars' fanciful homage to an ancient Roman marketplace

houses 160 designer emporia, including one-name catwalk wonders such as Armani, Gucci, Versace and DKNY; specialty boutiques such as fashionable Theory, Intermix and Scoop NYC; Kiehl's old-world apothecary and modern MAC cosmetics; and the Exotic Cars (p97) showroom.

GRAND CANAL SHOPPES
☎ 414-4500; www.thegrandcanal shoppes.com; Venetian, 3377 Las Vegas Blvd S; ⏲ 10am-11pm Sun-Thu, 10am-midnight Fri & Sat; Ⓜ Harrah's/Imperial Palace

Wandering minstrels, jugglers and laughable living statues perform at St Mark's Sq inside this Italianate mall. Cobblestone walkways wind past Burberry, Godiva, Kenneth Cole, Jimmy Choo, Sephora and 80 other luxury shops. The doors are thrown open for early-bird window shopping at 7am. Don't want to walk? Take a leisurely gondola ride (p84).

HARD ROCK
☎ 693-5000; www.hardrockhotel.com; Hard Rock, 4455 Paradise Rd; ⏲ most shops 10am-11pm Sun-Thu, 10am-2am Fri & Sat; 🚌 108, 202

For pop-star clothing brands and rare rock 'n' roll collectibles, hit this off-Strip casino's logo shop. Pop into Love Jones for imported lingerie and Rocks, a 24-hour

jewelry store, to pick up that diamond watch right after your big win at the poker tables.

MANDALAY PLACE
☎ 632-7777; www.mandalaybay.com; skybridge btwn Mandalay Bay & Luxor, 3930 Las Vegas Blvd S; ⏲ 10am-11pm Sun-Thu, 10am-midnight Fri & Sat; 🚌 Deuce

With a de-stress atmosphere and vaulted ceilings, M-Bay's airy promenade shows off 40 unique,

Stroll the length of the Miracle Mile Shops (p94)

fashion-forward boutiques, including Fornarina for women, Elton's for men, the burlesque-inspired Champagne Suzy boutique, Urban Outfitters for tweens, Lush (p98), the Art of Shaving and the first-ever Nike Golf store.

MIRACLE MILE SHOPS
☎ 888-800-8284; www.miraclemile shopslv.com; Planet Hollywood, 3663 Las Vegas Blvd S; ⏰ 10am-11pm Sun-Thu, 11am-midnight Fri & Sat; Ⓜ Bally's/Paris

Measuring an incredible 1.5 miles long, this sleekly redesigned mall harbors 170 retailers and 15 restaurants. The focus is contemporary chains, especially urban apparel. Stand-out shops include Bettie Page for mid-20th-century vintage and pin-up styles, imports H&M and Ben Sherman, the LA denim king True Religion, and Stash, Vegas' own rock-star boutique.

SHOPPES AT PALAZZO
☎ 607-4300; www.palazzolasvegas .com; Palazzo, 3327 Las Vegas Blvd S; ⏰ 10am-11pm Sun-Thu, 10am-midnight Fri & Sat; Ⓜ Harrah's/Imperial Palace

Towered over by three-story Barneys New York department store, this casino mall is a glittering galaxy of fashion stars such as Diane von Furstenberg and

Cole Haan; London trendsetters Chloé and Thomas Pink; Canali for tailor-made Italian apparel; Annie Creamcheese for glam 20th-century mod fashions; Anya Hindmarch for handbags and accessories; and Manolo Blahnik for divine shoes.

TOWN SQUARE
☎ 269-5001; www.townsquarelas vegas.com; 6605 Las Vegas Blvd S; ⏰ 10am-9:30pm Mon-Thu, 10am-10pm Fri & Sat, 11am-8pm Sun; 🚌 Deuce

Within sight of McCarran International Airport, this polished outdoor mall lined with faux facades harbors sought-after chains such as Juicy Couture, Sephora, Apple, Abercrombie & Fitch and Metropark. Palm trees wave over pedestrian-only streets, while tasty restaurants and a state-of-the-art cinema draw in the crowds.

VIA BELLAGIO
☎ 693-7111; www.bellagio.com; Bellagio, 3600 Las Vegas Blvd S; ⏰ 10am-midnight; Ⓜ Bally's/Paris

Bellagio's swish indoor promenade is home to the who's who of fashion-plate designers: Prada, Armani, Gucci, Hermès, Yves Saint Laurent, Tiffany & Co and Fred Leighton (p89). Bring a pocket pooch and your darkest celebrity-in-disguise sunglasses.

SHOP > SPECIALIST STORES

V

LAS VEGAS

SHOP

🏯 WYNN ESPLANADE

☎ 770-7000; www.wynnlasvegas.com;
Wynn Las Vegas, 3131 Las Vegas Blvd S;
🕑 10am-11pm Sun-Thu, 10am-midnight
Fri & Sat; 🚌 Deuce

Steve Wynn's eponymous resort showcases 75,000 sq ft of consumer bliss, with top-of-the-line retailers such as Cartier, Hermès, Jean-Paul Gaultier and Oscar de la Renta, plus the high-tech toy store Gizmos. After you hit the jackpot, take a test drive at the Penske-Wynn Ferrari/Maserati dealership.

🛍 SPECIALIST STORES

Technorati gravitate toward the **Apple Store** (☎ 650-9550) at the Fashion Show (p92), **Sony Style** (☎ 697-5420) at the Forum Shops (p92) and superstore **Fry's Electronics** (☎ 932-1400; www.frys.com; 6845 Las Vegas Blvd S; 🕑 9am-9pm Mon-Sat, 9am-7pm Sun; 🚌 Deuce).

🏯 AUTO COLLECTIONS

☎ 794-3174; www.autocollections .com; Imperial Palace, 5th fl, 3535 Las Vegas Blvd S; adult/concession $7/3, free coupons on website; 🕑 9:30am-9:30pm; Ⓜ Harrah's/Imperial Palace

Car buffs could easily pass away hours drooling over one of the world's largest privately owned auto collections. Among the prized vehicles on hand here (some for sale) are more Bentleys and Dusenbergs than you could toss a chauffeur at, not to mention the classic '67 Ford Mustang from the movie *Gone in Sixty Seconds*.

LOW-ROLLER DEALS

Brand-name bargain hunters can save a lotta moolah at these jam-packed outlet malls:
Fashion Outlets Las Vegas (☎ 874-1400, 888-424-6898; www.fashionoutletlasvegas .com; 32100 Las Vegas Blvd S, off I-15 exit 1, Primm; 🕑 10am-8pm) At the Nevada/ California state line, about a 40-minute drive southwest of Las Vegas, discover a mix of more than 100 high-end (Burberry, Coach, Ralph Lauren, Versace, Neiman Marcus Last Call) and everyday (Banana Republic, Nike, Williams Sonoma) brands. It's accessible from the Strip via a shoppers' shuttle (round trip $15), but it's only worth the trip for Californians who already happen to be driving by.
Las Vegas Premium Outlets (☎ 474-7500; www.premiumoutlets.com; 875 S Grand Central Parkway; 🕑 10am-9pm Mon-Sat, 10am-8pm Sun; 🚌 108) The most upscale of Vegas' outlet malls features 120 high-end names like Armani Exchange, Calvin Klein, Coach, Dolce & Gabbana and Kenneth Cole, along with a few casual brands like Levi's. CAT's Downtown Shoppers Express shuttle serves the mall every 20 minutes from 10am until 5pm.

LAS VEGAS

SHOP

🏠 BASS PRO SHOPS OUTDOOR WORLD

☎ 730-5200; www.basspro.com; 8200 Dean Martin Dr; ⊙ 9am-10pm Mon-Sat, 10am-7pm Sun; 🚌 217

Keep an eye on the handcrafted wildlife chandeliers at this redneck superstore adjacent to the Silverton casino resort. Paradise for fishers and hunters, Bass Pro stakes its claim on a ginormous showroom with a rock-climbing wall, an indoor archery range, a 40,000-gallon aquarium and a meandering stream stocked with native Nevada species.

🏠 CASA FUENTE

☎ 731-5051; Forum Shops at Caesars Palace, 3500 Las Vegas Blvd S; ⊙ 10am-11pm Sun-Thu, 10am-midnight Fri & Sat; Ⓜ Flamingo/Caesars Palace

A million-dollar cigar shop with a bar that feels like a little slice of Havana: the walk-in humidor contains signature stogies from the Dominican Republic (not Cuba, though – damn those US customs regulations!). Order a tropical cocktail from the petite bar, then grab a wicker chair out front.

Cocktails and cigars – a winning combination at Casa Fuente

⬚ DESERT ROCK SPORTS
☎ 254-1143; www.desertrocksportslv
.com; 8221 W Charleston Blvd, west of
S Buffalo Dr; 🕑 9am-7pm Mon-Sat, 10am-
6pm Sun Oct-Mar, call for hr Apr-Sep;
🚌 206
Run by climbers, this outdoor-
adventure shop rents bouldering
crash pads and carries all-weather
apparel and brand-name hiking,
rock-climbing, camping and back-
packing equipment. The indoor
Red Rock Climbing Center (☎ 254-5604;
www.redrockclimbingcenter.com; 8201 W
Charleston Blvd) is next door.

⬚ DOUBLE HELIX
☎ 735-9463; www.palazzolasvegas
.com; Palazzo, 3327 Las Vegas Blvd S;
🕑 10am-11pm Sun-Thu, 10am-midnight
Fri & Sat; Ⓜ Harrah's/Imperial Palace
At this wine boutique, exclusive
bottles are stacked higher than
poker chips on a WSOP final table.
Knowledgeable staff escort oenophiles through the VIP room and
proffer champagne flights outside
at the tasting bar, which dispenses
rare vintages by the glass.

⬚ EXOTIC CARS
☎ 893-4800; www.ecacp.com; Forum
Shops at Caesars Palace, 3500 Las Vegas
Blvd S; 🕑 10am-11pm Sun-Thu, 10am-
midnight Fri & Sat; Ⓜ Flamingo/Caesars
Palace
More of an attraction than a
bi-level retail shop, here you can
peruse Porsche-brand apparel, get
your photo taken inside a Ferrari
and salivate over a racier lifestyle.
Dozens of rare imported vehicles
are on display, from Aston Martins
to Lamborghinis, some easily
worth up to a million dollars.

⬚ FIELD OF DREAMS
☎ 792-8233; www.fieldofdreams.com;
Forum Shops at Caesars Palace, 3500 Las
Vegas Blvd S; 🕑 10am-11pm Sun-Thu,
10am-midnight Fri & Sat; Ⓜ Flamingo/
Caesars Palace
The first name in sports and
celebrity memorabilia in Las
Vegas, Field of Dreams deserves
a look whether you're interested
in buying or not. Among the
items that have been sold here
are a baseball autographed and
inscribed with an apology by dis-
graced baseball legend Pete Rose,
who sometimes makes in-store
appearances.

⬚ GYPSY CARAVAN ANTIQUE VILLAGE
☎ 868-3302; 1302 S 3rd St; 🕑 10am-
5pm Tue-Sat; 🚌 108, Deuce
One person's trash truly is another
person's treasure, as the saying
goes. Helter-skelter shops inside
this shabby-chic collection of
houses are filled with affordable
treasures, especially for fans of
outrageous kitsch and funky
fashions.

☐ HOUDINI'S MAGIC SHOP
☎ 798-4789; www.houdini.com; Forum Shops at Caesars Palace, 3500 Las Vegas Blvd S; ⏱ 10am-11pm Sun-Thu, 10am-midnight Fri & Sat; Ⓜ Flamingo/Caesars Palace

The legendary escape artist's legacy lives on at this shop packed with gags, pranks and magic tricks. Tuxedoed magicians perform for free, and every purchase includes a free private lesson in the secretive back room. Look over the shop's mini museum of authentic Houdini memorabilia, including handcuffs.

☐ LUSH
☎ 227-5874; www.mandalaybay.com; Mandalay Place, 3930 Las Vegas Blvd S; ⏱ 10am-11pm Sun-Thu, 10am-midnight Fri & Sat; 🚍 Deuce

Be deliciously immersed back in your hotel room's bathtub with Lush's essential oil–infused 'bath ballistics,' bubble bars and cocoa-butter bath melts, not to mention fresh, handmade pots of balms, cleansers and massage bars. Mostly natural and often organic, this is an eco-green beauty queen's dream.

☐ MAIN STREET ANTIQUES
☎ 382-1882; www.mainstreetantiqueslv.com; 500 S Main St; ⏱ 9am-6pm; 🚍 108

Stranded in the Naked City, this one-stop retro extravaganza with over 40 different dealers

is a primo place for picking up vintage Vegas souvenirs, from gaming chips to casino-hotel ashtrays and matchbooks. Keep a sharp eye out for retro Rat Pack memorabilia, too.

☐ NIKETOWN
☎ 650-8888; www.nike.com; Forum Shops at Caesars Palace, 3500 Las Vegas Blvd S; ⏱ 10am-11pm Sun-Thu, 10am-midnight Fri & Sat; Ⓜ Flamingo/Caesars Palace

The sporty kicks might not help you jump like Air Jordan, but they will certainly send your credit-card bill soaring. A sociable running club convenes here every Wednesday at 6pm. For couch-potato sports fans, the big-league memorabilia and big-screen TVs are worth a look.

☐ WEIRD & WONDERFUL

You can find quirky Atomic Age collectibles, books and movies at the Atomic Testing Museum (p74). Swoon over candelabras and life-sized photos of the legend himself at the Liberace Museum (p79).

☐ BONANZA GIFTS
☎ 385-7359; www.worldslargestgiftshop.com; 2440 Las Vegas Blvd S; ⏱ 8am-midnight; Ⓜ Sahara

It's not the 'World's Largest Gift Shop' as it claims to be, but the truly terrible and guaranteed 100%

BEST ONLY-IN-VEGAS SHOPS
> Gamblers Book Shop (p90)
> Gamblers General Store (below)
> Houdini's Magic Shop (opposite)
> Rainbow Feather Dyeing Co (right)
> Showcase Slots (right)

tacky selection of only-in-Vegas souvenirs includes entire aisles of dice clocks, snow globes, slogan T-shirts, shot glasses and XXX gags. Beware that prices are higher here than downtown on Fremont St.

☐ GAMBLERS GENERAL STORE
☎ 382-9903, 800-322-2447; www .gamblersgeneralstore.com; 800 S Main St; ☿ 9am-6pm; ☐ 108
This authentic store has it all, from custom-made chips to roulette wheels and poker tables identical to those found in many casinos, plus Nevada's largest inventory of slot machines. It's perfect for cheapo gifts like decks of cards once used in real-life Vegas casinos.

☐ GUN STORE
☎ 454-1110; www.thegunstorelas vegas.com; 2900 E Tropicana Ave; ☿ 9am-6:30pm; ☐ 201
Attention wannabe action heroes. If you're dying to fire off a sub-machine gun or feel the heft of a Beretta, Colt or Glock in your hot little hands, visit this high-powered shop with an indoor video training range. Tuesday is ladies' day.

☐ RAINBOW FEATHER DYEING CO
☎ 598-0988; www.rainbowfeatherco .com; 1036 S Main St; ☿ 9am-4pm Mon-Fri, 9am-1pm Sat; ☐ 108
Where to satisfy that boa fetish? Need turkey, chicken, duck, goose, pheasant, ostrich or peacock quills? Rainbow stocks a positively fabulous selection of fine feathers and showgirl fans in every possible hue.

☐ SERGE'S SHOWGIRL WIGS
☎ 732-1015, 800-947-9447; www.show girlwigs.com; Commercial Center, 953 E Sahara Ave; ☿ 10am-5:30pm Mon-Sat; ☐ 204
In a trashy strip mall east of the Sahara casino hotel, Serge's friendly staff of stylists help Vegas showgirls and drag queens (and even little ol' you) find their inner glamour girl.

☐ SHOWCASE SLOTS
☎ 888-522-7568; www.showcaseslots .com; Miracle Mile Shops, 3663 Las Vegas Blvd S; ☿ 10am-11pm Sun-Thu, 10am-midnight Fri & Sat; Ⓜ Bally's/Paris
Sock away spare change in your own stylish piggy bank: buy a vintage or modern 'one-armed bandit' or video-poker machine. It sells roulette wheels and Elvis-emblazoned packs of playing cards, too. Also at Town Square (p94).

🍴 EAT

Sin City is studded with star chefs, and today's foodie scene is on fire. The recent invasion of the Strip by French chefs, most notably Guy Savoy and Joël Robuchon, is just the latest notch in the city's climb toward ever more sophisticated epicurean experiences.

After Wolfgang Puck brought Spago to Caesars Palace in 1992, celebrity American chefs opened branches at every megaresort. Geniuses of the kitchen who have leapt onto the Strip include Emeril Legasse, Mario Batali, Michael Mina, David Burke, Bobby Flay and Charlie Trotter. However, cheap buffets and meal deals still exist, mostly downtown and at less glitzy Strip addresses.

Every major casino hotel has a 24-hour café, typically offering graveyard specials after midnight. Weekend champagne brunch buffets (8am to 3pm) are a hot ticket. Lunch is between 11:30am and 2:30pm. Dinner is from 5pm to 10pm Sunday through Thursday, and to 11pm on Friday and Saturday nights.

Almost every restaurant menu on the Strip offers a few creative vegetarian appetizers and side dishes, which you can easily combine into a full meal. Restaurants with a particularly good vegetarian selection have been identified in the individual reviews with the symbol **V** .

Book tables as far in advance as you can for pricier restaurants. Reservations at the biggest names are crucial, especially on weekends. At the most famous places, jackets may be required for men. **OpenTable** (www .opentable.com) is a free online booking service. Immediate bar seating is often available.

The standard gratuity is 15% to 20% before tax. A service charge of 15% to 18% is often added for groups of six or more; don't double-tip.

Top Left Get your burgers fresh at Stripburger (p105) **Bottom Left** Don't mess around with the hefty sandwiches at Canter's Deli (p115)

LAS VEGAS

EAT

THE STRIP
For tips on Vegas' belly-busting buffets, turn to p171.

 BELLAGIO

The Bellagio's stable of culinary heavyweights has started showing its age. For reservations, visit www.bellagio.com or call ☎ 877-234-6358. Note that children are not permitted at many restaurants.

THE BUFFET
Buffet $$

☎ 693-7111; Bellagio, 3600 Las Vegas Blvd S; 🕒 7-11am & 11am-4pm Mon-Fri, 4-10pm Sun-Thu, gourmet dinner 4-10pm Fri-Sat, brunch 7am-4pm Sat & Sun; Ⓜ Bally's/Paris; Ⓥ ♿

The Bellagio competes for top honors for Vegas' best live-action buffet. The sumptuous all-you-can-eat spread includes seafood and uncountable creative dishes from all around the globe. Go for lunch, which is the best value.

FIX
Modern American $$

☎ 693-8400; www.lightgroup.com; Bellagio, 3600 Las Vegas Blvd S; 🕒 5pm-midnight; Ⓜ Bally's/Paris

It's a perfect pre-clubbing launch pad, or just the venue for eyeing celebs and the casino floor. This trendy, high-flying kitchen makes

gourmet comfort-food goodies such as lobster tacos, Kobe beef sliders with spiced fries and choco-java 'shake & cake.' Reservations recommended at Fix and its sister Japanese restaurant and sushi bar Yellowtail.

JEAN-PHILIPPE PATISSERIE
French $

☎ 693-7111; Spa Tower, Bellagio, 3600 Las Vegas Blvd S; items $5-10; 🕒 7am-11pm Sun-Thu, 7am-midnight Fri & Sat; Ⓜ Bally's/Paris

The world's largest chocolate fountain cascades inside this champion pastrymaker's shop, known for its fantastic sorbets, gelatos and chocolate confections. Sugar-free sweets don't disappoint either.

OLIVES
Mediterranean $$

☎ 693-8181; www.toddenglish.com; Via Bellagio, Bellagio, 3600 Las Vegas Blvd S; 🕒 11am-3pm & 5-10:30pm; Ⓜ Bally's/Paris; Ⓥ

East Coast chef Todd English pays homage to the ancient

life-giving fruit. Flatbread pizzas, housemade pastas and flame-licked meats get top billing. The chef's table faces a bustling open kitchen, while the patio tables overlook Lake Como. There's a good wine list, and flamboyant desserts. Reservations here are necessary.

🍴 PICASSO
Mediterranean $$$
☎ 693-7223; Via Bellagio, Bellagio, 3600 Las Vegas Blvd S; ⏰ 6-9:30pm Wed-Mon; Ⓜ Bally's/Paris
Five-star chef Julian Serrano delivers artistic Franco-Iberian fusion in a museum-like setting. Original Picasso masterpieces regrettably overshadow entrées such as the signature sautéed fallow deer medallions or seafood *boudin* that appear on prix-fixe dinner menus ($115 to $150). Linger on the lakeside patio over a *digestif*. Jacket and tie are suggested. Reservations are essential.

🍴 CAESARS PALACE & FORUM SHOPS
Make reservations for dining with the gods at www.caesarspalace .com, or call ☎ 731-7731 or ☎ 877-346-4642. Wolfgang Puck's Spago ($$) is inside the Forum Shops (p92).

🍴 BOA STEAKHOUSE
Steakhouse/Seafood $$
☎ 733-7373; www.boasteak.com/ balboa; 3rd fl, Forum Shops, Caesars Palace, 3500 Las Vegas Blvd S; ⏰ noon-10pm Sun-Thu, noon-11:30pm Fri & Sat; Ⓜ Flamingo/Caesars Palace
Boa, structured with stainless steel and Zen-like tree branches, first made its name in mixology. The prime cuts of steak with your choice of rubs, crusts and sauces, plus top-grade seafood flown in from the coast, are just as prize-worthy. Reservations recommended.

🍴 BRADLEY OGDEN
Modern American $$$
☎ 731-7413; www.larkcreek.com/bolv; opposite Colosseum, Caesars Palace, 3570 Las Vegas Blvd S; ⏰ 5-11pm; Ⓜ Flamingo/Caesars Palace
With farm-fresh fare, this restaurant delivers nouveau takes on American classics, such as blue-cheese souf-flés, bison tenderloin and New England crab with dollops of coconut foam. Reservations advised.

🍴 CYPRESS STREET MARKET PLACE
Fast Food $
☎ 731-7110; opposite Colosseum, Caesars Palace, 3570 Las Vegas Blvd S; ⏰ 11am-11pm; Ⓜ Flamingo/Caesars Palace; Ⓥ ♿
Conveniently charge those fresh, made-to-order pizzas and salads,

global wraps, Asian stir-fries and southern barbecue, along with beer, wine and health drinks, to a 'smart' card, then pay upon exiting. Courtyard tables perch happily over the casino floor.

🍴 MESA GRILL
Southwestern $$
☎ 731-7731; www.mesagrill.com/las vegas; opposite Colosseum, Caesars Palace, 3570 Las Vegas Blvd S; ⏲ 11am-2:30pm Mon-Fri, 10:30am-3pm Sat & Sun, 5-11pm daily; Ⓜ Flamingo/Caesars Palace; Ⓥ
While the star New York chef doesn't cook on the premises, his bold signature menu of Southwestern fusion fare lives up to the hype, whether it's a sweet potato tamale with crushed pecan butter, blue corn pancakes or spice-rubbed pork tenderloin.

🍴 PAYARD BISTRO
French $$
☎ 731-7292; www.payard.com; Caesars Palace, 3570 Las Vegas Blvd S; ⏲ 6:30am-3pm; Ⓜ Flamingo/Caesars Palace
Third-generation chef and chocolatier Françoise Payard recreates classic French bistro tastes as rich as the handcrafted woodwork, leather banquettes and crystal chandelier in the bright dining room. Out front is a divine **pâtisserie** (⏲ 6:30am-11pm) and espresso bar for quick pick-me-ups.

🍴 RAO'S
Italian $$
☎ 731-7267; www.raos.com; Caesars Palace, 3570 Las Vegas Blvd S; ⏲ 5-11pm; Ⓜ Flamingo/Caesars Palace
One person's heavenly meatball is another's bland hunk of meat: that's the lesson at the overhyped Vegas version of East Harlem's legendary 10-table restaurant, dating from 1896. Here the homestyle fare gets only mixed reviews, despite the polished red-and-black dining rooms and poolside patio by the outdoor bocce court.

🍴 RESTAURANT GUY SAVOY
French $$$
☎ 731-7286; www.guysavoy.com; 2nd fl, Augustus Tower, Caesars Palace, 3570 Las Vegas Blvd S; ⏲ 5:30-10:30pm Wed-Sun; Ⓜ Flamingo/Caesars Palace
With Strip-view windows overlooking Caesars' Roman Plaza, this intimate dining room is the only US endeavor of three-star Michelin chef Guy Savoy. Both the culinary concepts and the prices reach heavenly heights.

HIGH-ROLLER TABLES ON THE STRIP
> Alex (p117)
> Restaurant Guy Savoy (above)
> Tao (p117)
> Joël Robuchon (p108)
> Restaurant Charlie (p112)

Pop by the Bubble Bar for champagne flights and delicate small plates such as artichoke and black truffle soup. Jacket and tie required. Reservations essential but difficult to get.

🍴 TREVI
Italian $$

☎ 735-4663; www.trevi-italian.com; **Forum Shops, Caesars Palace, 3500 Las Vegas Blvd S;** ⏱ 11am-11pm; Ⓜ Flamingo/Caesars Palace

Formerly Bertolini's, this fountain-side trattoria races ahead of the pack with wood-fired pizzas, fresh specialty pastas, Italian sodas and 'sorbetini' cocktails. It has a convivial atmosphere and attentive service.

🍴 FASHION SHOW

For authentic Italian-style scoops, rainbow-colored Gelato Cafe ($) is a sweet spot.

🍴 CAFE BA-BA-REEBA!
Spanish $$

☎ 258-1211; www.cafebabareeba.com; street level, Fashion Show, 3200 Las Vegas Blvd S; ⏱ 11:30am-11pm Sun-Thu, 11:30am-midnight Fri & Sat; 🚌 Deuce

At this enticing Spanish tapas bar-bistro, attentive staff present paellas for two and a parade of authentic hot and cold tapas such as *patatas aioli* (garlic potatoes),

brochetas (meat/seafood skewers), spicy *gambas* (shrimp) and imported cheeses. Uniquely flavored sangrias and bite-sized desserts tempt.

🍴 CAPITAL GRILLE
Steakhouse/Seafood $$

☎ 932-6631; www.thecapitalgrille.com; 3rd fl, Fashion Show, 3200 Las Vegas Blvd S; ⏱ 11:30am-10:30pm Mon-Fri, noon-10:30pm Sat, 4-10pm Sun; 🚌 Deuce

What sets this clubby, chain steak-house apart is hand-cut, dry-aged beef, carved chops and succulent seafood. For a posh power lunch, order a ribeye-steak sandwich with caramelized onions or a lobster-crab burger. The Old and New World wine list gets the nod from *Wine Spectator*.

🍴 STRIPBURGER
American $

☎ 737-8747; www.lasvegasstrip burger.com; street level, Fashion Show, 3200 Las Vegas Blvd S; ⏱ 11:30am-1am Sun-Thu, 11:30am-2am Fri & Sat; 🚌 Deuce; ♿

A shiny, silver-roofed open-air diner in the round serves up all-natural beef, chicken, tuna and veggie burgers, with chili-spiked 'atomic' cheese fries on the side. Draft microbrews, thick milk-shakes and chocolate cake are served, too.

🍴 LUXOR

For a zingy, fusion-flavored meal in sexy surrounds, queue for celeb chef Kerry Simon's CatHouse ($$).

🍴 COMPANY AMERICAN BISTRO
Modern American $$

☎ 262-4702; www.luxor.com; Luxor, 3900 Las Vegas Blvd S; 🕑 5-10:30pm Sun-Thu, 5-11:30pm Fri & Sat; 🚌 Deuce
Make a foray into fashion-plate dining in a cozy faux-ski chalet and fireside lounge. Meaty mains, such as soul-food buttermilk fried chicken with waffles, or pork schnitzel with fried egg and brown-butter sauce, are worth the wait. Fawning service relentlessly pushes wine pairings for each course, but stick to your guns and order more modestly. Reservations recommended.

🍴 MANDALAY BAY & MANDALAY PLACE

For table reservations, click to www.mandalaybay.com or call ☎ 632-7200.

🍴 AUREOLE
Modern American $$$

☎ 632-7401; www.aureolelv.com; Mandalay Bay, 3950 Las Vegas Blvd S; 🕑 6-10:30pm, wine-tower lounge 6pm-midnight; 🚌 Deuce
Chef Charlie Palmer's seasonally inspired tasting menus (from $95), which show off dishes like saffron seafood chowder and maple-nut baklava, are not

Dine with the fashionable set at Company American Bistro

always artfully executed. But it's worth ordering wine just to watch catsuit-clad 'wine angels' ascend the four-story tower. Extensive wine list, upscale dress. Reservations essential.

🍴 BURGER BAR
American $$

☎ 632-9364; www.fleurdelyssf.com; Mandalay Place, 3930 Las Vegas Blvd S; 🕐 10am-11pm Sun, 10:30am-11pm Mon-Thu, 10:30am-2am Fri & Sat; 🚍 Deuce; ♿

Since when is a hamburger worth $60? When it's built with Kobe beef, sautéed foie gras, shaved truffles and Madeira sauce (sounds messy, and it *is*). Build your own beef, buffalo, turkey or veggie burger for much less, then polish off a microbrew and bite into a whimsical dessert.

🍴 CHINA GRILL
Chinese Fusion $$

☎ 632-7404; www.chinagrillmanage ment.com/chinaLV; Mandalay Bay, 3950 Las Vegas Blvd S; 🕐 5:30pm-midnight; 🚍 Deuce

In chic surrounds, Marco Polo–inspired takes on traditional themes create neo-Asian delights like lobster pancakes and sake-marinated 'drunken' chicken. Family-sized dishes are for sharing. Infamously indiscreet unisex 'garden' bath-

rooms were designed by Jeffrey Beers. Reservations suggested.

🍴 FLEUR DE LYS
French $$$

☎ 632-9400; www.fleurdelyssf.com; Mandalay Bay, 3950 Las Vegas Blvd S; 🕐 5:30-10:30pm; 🚍 Deuce

Overseen by French chef Hubert Keller of San Francisco's famous Fleur de Lys, this soaring space that's outfitted with European linens and flower-patterned china enhances the thoughtful seasonal tasting menus (vegetarians OK). Expect flawless service and expert cuisine such as artisan foie gras, grilled diver scallops and eggplant caviar. Reservations recommended.

🍴 RM SEAFOOD
Seafood $$$

☎ 632-9300; www.rmseafood.com; Mandalay Place, 3930 Las Vegas Blvd S; 🕐 restaurant 5:30-10pm, café 11am-4pm daily, 5-10:30pm Sun-Thu, 5-11:30pm Fri & Sat; 🚍 Deuce

New York chef Rick Moonen takes a dual approach to the sustainable catch of the day. Upstairs in the restaurant, relish haute American seafood dinners. The downstairs café, furnished with rich mahogany booths, offers a more expansive menu, a raw shellfish and sushi bar, and a unique 'biscuit bar' serving warm seafood salads.

BEST STEAKHOUSES

Vegas has hundreds of places to get a hunk of burnin' red meat. Extra props go to the following steakhouses:
> Cut (Palazzo; p111)
> Craftsteak (MGM Grand; right)
> Boa Steakhouse (Forum Shops; p103)
> N9NE (Palms; p127)
> Envy (Renaissance; p121)

STRIPSTEAK
Steakhouse/Seafood $$$

☎ 632-7414; www.michaelmina.net; Mandalay Bay, 3950 Las Vegas Blvd S; 🕒 5:30-10:30pm; 🚌 Deuce
Famed for his seafood restaurants, chef Michael Mina has made a graceful debut into the cut-throat world of Vegas steakhouses. Here minimalist modern design is warmed by earth tones, and an exceptional menu of Angus and Kobe beef delightfully detours from tradition, with the likes of duck fat fries, spicy green-papaya salad and tomato-dusted red-onion rings on the side. Reservations recommended.

🍴 MGM GRAND

For reservations, click to www.mgmgrand.com or call ☎ 877-793-7111. Palatable options include Fiamma Trattoria & Bar ($$) for modish Italian, and polished Pearl ($$$) for Chinese.

CRAFTSTEAK
Steakhouse/Seafood $$$

☎ 891-7318; www.craftrestaurant.com; Studio Walk, MGM Grand, 3799 Las Vegas Blvd S; 🕒 5:30-10pm Sun-Thu, 5:30-10:30pm Fri & Sat; Ⓜ MGM Grand
What this contemporary, richly wood-laden space may lack in exclusivity it makes up for with an intriguing menu of grass-fed vs grain-fed strip steaks, grilled bison, braised duck confit and a bounty from the sea: regional American oysters, Russian caviar and Australian lobster tail. There's a three-course tasting menu from $100.

JOËL ROBUCHON
French $$$

☎ 891-7925; www.joel-robuchon .com; MGM Grand, 3799 Las Vegas Blvd S; 🕒 5:30-10pm Sun-Thu, 5:30-10:30pm Fri & Sat; Ⓜ MGM Grand
The acclaimed 'Chef of the Century' leads the pack in the French invasion of Las Vegas. Adjacent to the Mansion, a high-rollers' gaming area, plush dining rooms done up in leather and velvet imitate 1930s Paris. There are complex seasonal tasting menus ($250 to $325). Reservations essential but difficult to get. At less-expensive L'Atelier de Joël Robuchon ($$$) next door, bar seats front an exhibition kitchen.

🍴 SEABLUE
Seafood $$$
☎ 891-3486; www.michaelmina.net;
MGM Grand, 3799 Las Vegas Blvd S;
🕑 5:30-10pm Sun-Thu, 5:30-10:30pm
Fri & Sat; Ⓜ MGM Grand
Anything from Nantucket Bay
scallops to Gulf shrimp to Manila
clams comes raw, fried, steamed
and roasted out of two exhibition
kitchens. Create your own mix-
and-match salads from a long list
of farm-fresh ingredients, and then
swallow a fanciful lobster corn dog.

🍴 SHIBUYA
Japanese $$$
☎ 891-3001; Studio Walk, MGM Grand,
3799 Las Vegas Blvd S; 🕑 5-10pm Sun-
Thu, 5-10:30pm Fri & Sat; Ⓜ MGM Grand
A stellar sake cellar, art spreading
behind the sushi bar and tastebud-
awakening appetizers, such as
garlic-rubbed yellowtail with citrus
juice and black-truffle oil, and
oysters spiked with *ponzu* sauce.
Teppanyaki set menus come with
lobster-miso or mushroom soup.

🍴 'WICHCRAFT
Deli $
☎ 891-3166; www.craftrestaurant.com;
Studio Walk, MGM Grand, 3799 Las Vegas
Blvd S; 🕑 10am-6pm Sun-Thu, 10am-
8pm Fri & Sat; Ⓜ MGM Grand; Ⓥ ♿
This bewitching kitchen serves
belly-warming sandwiches such as
grilled cheddar with smoked ham
and baked apples, and chicken
salad with roasted tomatoes on a
baguette. Side salads and fruit are
as fun as the whoopie-pie desserts.

🍴 WOLFGANG PUCK BAR & GRILL
Italian $$
☎ 891-3000; www.wolfgangpuck
.com; MGM Grand, 3799 Las Vegas Blvd S;
🕑 11:30am-10:30pm Sun-Thu, 11:30am-
11:30pm Fri & Sat; Ⓜ MGM Grand; Ⓥ
California flair pervades this ultra-
contemporary bistro just off the
casino floor. The truffled potato
chips with blue cheese, skirt steak
skewers with celery salad, wood-
fired pizzas and ricotta gnocchi
with sweet fennel sausage thrill,
just like the New World wine list.

🍴 MIRAGE
For reservations, go to www.mirage
.com or call ☎ 866-339-4566. Some
savory options include Stack ($$$),
the look-alike of Fix (p102), and
Carnegie Deli ($$), where every-
thing comes hugely oversized.

🍴 BLT BURGER
American $
☎ 792-7888; www.bltburger.com;
Mirage, 3400 Las Vegas Blvd S; 🕑 11am-
2am Sun & Tue-Wed, 10am-4am Mon &
Thu-Sat; Ⓜ Harrah's/Imperial Palace
Here, French-trained NYC chef
Laurent Tourondel grills up haute

LAS VEGAS

EAT

Black Angus beef, lamb and veggie burgers with all the trimmings, plus there are almost three dozen microbrews, liqueur-spiked 'adult' milkshakes, crisp sweet-potato fries and peanut-buttery s'mores for dessert. Beautiful mod diner-style furnishings have a background of enormous black-and-white photo murals that show off Nevada's desert and snowy mountains.

🍴 FIN
Chinese $$

☎ 791-7111; Mirage, 3400 Las Vegas Blvd S; 🕐 11am-3pm & 5-11pm; Ⓜ Harrah's/Imperial Palace

With ocean-colored glass baubles strung from the ceiling, this Chinese dining room feels like a glorious fishbowl. Perch regally while being surrounded by hand-painted silk wallpaper and feast on sophisticated classic to creative Chinese cuisine that is fit for an empress. Seafood delights are remarkably fresh; dim sum is served daily.

🍴 NEW YORK–NEW YORK

Dig into upscale country Irish cooking at Nine Fine Irishmen ($$). Upstairs on the mezzanine level is a cluster of fast-food stands: Nathan's famous hot dogs, Schrafft's ice cream, Tropicana juice smoothies and 99¢ cups of coffee.

🍴 IL FORNAIO
Italian $$

☎ 650-6500; www.ilfornaio.com; New York–New York, 3790 Las Vegas Blvd S; 🕐 7:30-10:30am daily, 11:30am-midnight Sun-Thu, 11:30am-1am Fri & Sat; Ⓜ MGM Grand; Ⓥ

Feast on wood-fired pizzas, salads and pastas, or make a meal of the antipasti platter with scallops wrapped in pancetta, baked eggplant, truffled cheeses and more. Delectable, fresh-baked breakfast goodies such as lemon-pecan scones are also available at **Il Fornaio Paneterria** (🕐 6am-7:30pm), near the hotel lobby.

🍴 VILLAGE EATERIES
Fast Food $

☎ 740-6969; www.nynyhotelcasino.com; New York–New York, 3790 Las Vegas Blvd S; 🕐 daily, hours vary; Ⓜ MGM Grand; Ⓥ

The cobblestone streets of NY–NY's imitation Greenwich Village are bursting with tasty, wallet-saving options: Greenberg & Sons Deli, authentic down to the egg-cream sodas; Fulton's Fish Frye for fish and chips; Gonzalez Y Gonzalez, a tequila-soaked Tex-Mex cantina; and Chin Chin Café, serving dim sum in the morning, and vegetarian tofu and other quick-fix dishes all day.

Savor the spiciness of Dos Caminos

 PALAZZO

For reservations, click to www
.palazzolasvegas.com or call
☎ 607-4300.

CUT

Steakhouse $$$

☎ 607-6300; www.wolfgangpuck.com;
Shoppes at Palazzo, 3327 Las Vegas
Blvd S; ⏰ 5:30-10pm Sun-Thu, 5:30-
11pm Fri & Sat, lounge 5pm-1am Mon-
Thu, 3pm-1am Fri-Sun; Ⓜ Harrah's/
Imperial Palace

Peripatetic Wolfgang Puck strikes
again, and this time he's on fire –
it's 1200°F in the broiler, to be
exact. Modern earth-toned
furnishings with stainless-steel
accents and dried-flower arrange-
ments complement a surprisingly
smart menu, which dares to infuse
Indian spices into Kobe beef, and
accompanies Nebraska corn-fed
steaks with Argentinean chimi-
churri sauce or Point Reyes blue
cheese. Reservations essential.

DOS CAMINOS

Mexican $$

☎ 577-9600; www.brguestrestaurants
.com; Palazzo, 3325 Las Vegas Blvd S;
⏰ 11am-11pm; Ⓜ Harrah's/Imperial
Palace

Whether you've got a boisterous
party or an intimate date, this sex-
ily reinvented Mexican restaurant
is the ideal place for lounging,

with its low-slung tables and sofas and a long list of specialty cocktails and tequila flights. Linger over *queso* fondues, spicy seafood ceviche and chili-rubbed meats *a la parilla* (from the grill). Weekend brunch brings tacos, *huevos* (eggs) and blueberry-corn pancakes.

🍴 ESPRESSAMENTE ILLY
Fast Food $

☎ 869-2233; www.palazzolasvegas
.com; Shoppes at Palazzo, 3327 Las Vegas Blvd S; ☽ 6am-midnight Sun-Thu, 6am-1am Fri & Sat; Ⓜ Harrah's/Imperial Palace

A whiff of real Italian espresso leads you inside this brightly lit café. House-made panini, dessert crepes and over four dozen flavors of artisan gelato provide the sugar rush you'll need to attack the racks nearby at Barneys New York (p94). Beware of the annoying, hidden 'dine-in' surcharge.

🍴 MORELS
Steakhouse/Seafood $$$

☎ 607-6333; www.palazzolasvegas
.com; Palazzo, 3325 Las Vegas Blvd S; ☽ 11am-11pm Mon-Thu, 11am-midnight Fri, 8am-midnight Sat, 8am-10pm Sun; Ⓜ Harrah's/Imperial Palace

Another LA imported steakhouse, bejeweled Morels has a few secret weapons: gorgeous alfresco patio seating elevated above the Strip, an ice seafood bar, an artisanal

cheese and charcuterie meat bar and a wine-dispensing system that lets you sip just a glass of thousand-dollar French and Californian vintages. Impeccable service. Reservations recommended.

🍴 RESTAURANT CHARLIE
Seafood $$$

☎ 607-6336; www.charlietrotters
.com; Palazzo, 3325 Las Vegas Blvd S; ☽ 5-10pm Sun-Thu, 5-11pm Fri & Sat; Ⓜ Harrah's/Imperial Palace

A bright beacon on the casino floor, chef Charlie Trotter's restaurant looks almost like a springtime garden in the desert. Choose from a hot-and-cold menu of luxury seafood in the sophisticated main dining room, or worship at the holy grail of the 18-seat Bar Charlie for exquisite tasting menus of sushi with a serious twist. Reservations essential.

🍴 SUSHISAMBA
Japanese/South American $$

☎ 607-0700; www.sushisamba.com; Shoppes at Palazzo, 3327 Las Vegas Blvd S; ☽ 11am-midnight Mon-Wed, 11am-1am Thu-Sat, 10am-midnight Sun, late-night menu till 4am daily; Ⓜ Harrah's/Imperial Palace

With the flouncy colors of Rio and martial-arts flicks digitally projected onto the walls, SushiSamba presents a chic, sleek integration of Peruvian,

LAS VEGAS

EAT

Brazilian and Japanese cuisine, from flawlessly grilled robata and churrasco meats, marinated sashimi ceviche spiked with citrus and chilies, or delicately done tempura boxes with dipping sauces. And whoa, the sake list is encyclopedic. Reservations strongly recommended.

🍴 TABLE 10
Steakhouse/Seafood $$

☎ 607-6363; www.emerils.com; Shoppes at Palazzo, 3327 Las Vegas Blvd S; ⏱ 11am-11pm Sun-Thu, 11am-midnight Fri & Sat; Ⓜ Harrah's/Imperial Palace

Named after a prime spot at Emeril Legasse's flagship restaurant in N'awlins, Table 10 offers a New American take on classics such as lobster pot pie, spinach salad and dry-aged Angus ribeye steaks. Over-the-top desserts include sweet-potato cheesecake and Jamaican blue-mountain cof-

---

BEST TABLES WITH A VIEW

When the panorama is important and price is not, ascend to the Palms' **Alizé** (p125), Paris Las Vegas' **Eiffel Tower Restaurant** (right) or the Stratosphere Tower's **Top of the World** (p115). For open-air patios perched above the Strip, book a table at TI's **Social House** (p116) or **Morels** (opposite) at the Palazzo.

---

fee chocolate cake. Reservations recommended.

🍴 PARIS LAS VEGAS

Other options include the Rue de la Paix's La Creperie ($).

🍴 EIFFEL TOWER RESTAURANT
French $$$

☎ 948-6937; www.eiffeltowerrestaurant .com; Eiffel Tower, Paris Las Vegas, 3655 Las Vegas Blvd S; ⏱ 11am-2:30pm daily, 5-10:15pm Sun-Thu, 5-10:45pm Fri & Sat; Ⓜ Bally's/Paris

The adage about 'the better the view, the worse the food' doesn't necessarily apply here. Night views of the Strip and Bellagio's fountains are breathtaking – from the right table, that is. The chef's haute tasting menu is recommended, as is the Franco-phile wine list. Reservations necessary.

🍴 LE VILLAGE BUFFET
Buffet $$

☎ 946-7000; www.parislasvegas.com; Rue de la Paix, Paris Las Vegas, 3655 Las Vegas Blvd S; ⏱ 7am-10pm Sun-Thu, 7am-11pm Fri & Sat; Ⓜ Bally's/Paris; Ⓥ ♿

Fruit and cheeses, cracked crab legs and a toasty range of breads and pastries make this arguably the best-value buffet on the Strip. Distinct cooking stations are themed by France's various regions. Breakfasts are *magnifique*, especially the Sunday champagne brunch.

🍴 PLANET HOLLYWOOD & MIRACLE MILE SHOPS
Look out for LA cult fave Pink's ($) Hollywood hot-dog stand coming soon.

🍴 KOI
Sushi $$
☎ 454-4555; www.planethollywood resort.com; upstairs, Planet Hollywood, 3667 Las Vegas Blvd S; 🕑 5:30-11pm Sun-Wed, 5:30pm-midnight Thu-Sat; Ⓜ Bally's/Paris
Although the paparazzi won't lunge at you outside the front door like at the ubercool LA hot spot of the same name, this sushi bar is making waves in the desert (move over, Nobu). Bite into yellowtail carpaccio and down a blood-orange sunset cosmo cocktail.

🍴 SPICE MARKET BUFFET
Buffet $$
☎ 785-5555; www.planethollywood resort.com; downstairs, Planet Hollywood, 3667 Las Vegas Blvd S; 🕑 7-10:30am, 11am-3pm & 4-10pm; Ⓜ Bally's/Paris
Middle Eastern specialties are thrown into the global mix at this jewel of a five-star buffet, with delectable desserts. Attentive service and live-action cooking stations

justify the often very long waits to be seated.

🍴 STRIP HOUSE
Steakhouse/Seafood $$$
☎ 737-5200; www.planethollywood resort.com; upstairs, Planet Hollywood, 3667 Las Vegas Blvd S; 🕑 5-11pm Sun-Thu, 5pm-midnight Fri & Sat; Ⓜ Bally's/Paris
Boudoir lamps, leather banquettes and vintage erotic art prints set the mood at this sultry steakhouse, an aspiring celeb hang-out. Start off with the garlic bread and Gorgonzola fondue, then fork into the broiler steaks and attack the 24-layer chocolate cake. Eclectic, sommelier-inspired wine list. Reservations here are recommended.

🍴 TODAI
Seafood Buffet $$
☎ 892-0021; www.todai.com; Miracle Mile Shops, 3663 Las Vegas Blvd S, enter off Harmon Ave; 🕑 11:30am-2:30pm daily, 5:30-9:30pm Sun-Thu, 5:30-10pm Fri & Sat; Ⓜ Bally's/Paris; ♿
An awesome all-you-can-gorge spread of Japanese, Chinese and Korean fare features dozens of sushi selections, sizzling seafood and cool Asian salads. Lobster, shellfish and crab legs are added to the mix at dinnertime. Desserts rock.

LAS VEGAS

EAT

STRATOSPHERE

TOP OF THE WORLD
Continental $$$
☎ 380-7711; www.topoftheworldlv
.com; Stratosphere, 2000 Las Vegas
Blvd S; ☼ 11am-2:45pm daily, 5:30-
10:30pm Sun-Thu, 5:30-11pm Fri & Sat;
Ⓜ Sahara

While taking in the cloud-level
views at this dressy, revolving
romantic roost perched atop the
Stratosphere Tower (p84), relish
impeccable service and satisfying
if overpriced mains such as wild
king salmon or chateaubriand for
two. Reservations recommended
for lunch, required for dinner.
Excellent wine list.

TI (TREASURE ISLAND)

For reservations, visit www
.treasureisland.com or call ☎ 866-
286-3809. Phở at the Coffee Shop
($) preps Vietnamese noodle soup
that won't leave you hungry.

CANTER'S DELI
Jewish Deli $
☎ 894-7111; www.cantersdeli.com; TI
(Treasure Island), 3300 Las Vegas Blvd S;
☼ 11am-midnight; 🚌 Deuce
What did Canter's bring over the
state line from its landmark LA
delicatessen? You guessed it: the
infamously gruff service. Steal a
seat at the stainless-steel counter

or slide into a super-mod booth,
then settle back for authentic deli
fare that's almost as good as it gets.

ISLA MEXICAN KITCHEN
Mexican/Southwestern $$
☎ 894-7223; www.treasureisland.com;
TI (Treasure Island), 3300 Las Vegas Blvd S;
☼ 4-11pm Sun-Thu, 4pm-midnight Fri &
Sat; 🚌 Deuce
Bold art enlivens the walls of this
invention by Mexican-born chef
Richard Sandoval, who creates
a fusion of south-of-the-border
tastes, such as guacamole with a
twist of mint, and lobster spiked
with serrano chilies. Call on Isla's
tequila goddess to help decipher
the bounteous menu of agave
elixirs.

Sample deli favorites at Canter's

🍴 SOCIAL HOUSE
Pan-Asian $$

☎ 894-7223; www.socialhouselv.com; TI (Treasure Island), 3300 Las Vegas Blvd S; ⏲ 5pm-midnight, late-night menu midnight-2am Fri & Sat; 🚌 Deuce

This sushi and sake bar is designed for socializing. While the panko-crusted crab cakes and tamarind short ribs may not always hit the right note, the modern setting with shoji-papered windows and a Strip-view patio do. Incredible desserts will make you want to come back.

🍴 VENETIAN & GRAND CANAL SHOPPES

This bite of Italy offers a dizzying line-up of dining destinations, but not all excel. Reservations (☎ 877-883-6423; www.venetian.com) and formal dress are a must for fancier places. Canyon Ranch Café ($$) serves healthy cuisine at the spa (p148), while French-flavored Bouchon ($$) is popular for breakfast and weekend brunch.

🍴 B&B RISTORANTE
Italian $$$

☎ 266-9977; www.mariobatali.com; Venetian, 3355 Las Vegas Blvd S; ⏲ 5-11pm; Ⓜ Harrah's/Imperial Palace

From thriving Italian restaurateur and TV chef Mario Batali and his winemaking partner (the other 'B'),

this risk-taking restaurant delivers eccentric yet tantalizing dishes, such as beef-cheek ravioli, baby red-oak leaf salad with blood-orange dressing and lamb's brains with lemon and sage. Extravagant Eurocentric wine list. Reservations strongly recommended.

🍴 DAVID BURKE
Modern American $$

☎ 414-7111; www.davidburke .com; Venetian, 3355 Las Vegas Blvd S; ⏲ 11:30am-2:30pm daily, 5-10pm Sun-Thu, 5-11pm Fri & Sat, lounge 3pm-late daily; Ⓜ Harrah's/Imperial Palace

The whimsical presentation of tongue-in-cheek, globally flavored cuisine makes this under-the-radar find even more sweet. Unwind in a candy-flavored dining room or order from the full menu in the noisy lounge. Look for 'Burke in a box' ($35), a Japanese-inspired presentation of five appetizers made fresh daily. Reservations suggested.

🍴 POSTRIO
Italian $$

☎ 796-1110; www.wolfgangpuck.com; Grand Canal Shoppes, Venetian, 3377 Las Vegas Blvd S; ⏲ café 11:30am-10pm Sun-Thu, 11:30am-11pm Fri & Sat, restaurant 5-10pm Sun-Thu, 5-11pm Fri & Sat; Ⓜ Harrah's/Imperial Palace; Ⓥ

This offshoot of Wolfgang Puck's San Francisco original features playful signature dishes; devotees can't get enough of the wood oven–baked pizzas, pastas and rich desserts. Designed for people-watching, the patio always beats the stuffy restaurant. Interesting wine list.

TAO
Pan-Asian $$$

☎ 388-8338; www.taolasvegas.com; Grand Canal Shoppes, Venetian, 3377 Las Vegas Blvd S; 🕑 5pm-midnight Sun-Thu, 5pm-1am Fri & Sat; Ⓜ Harrah's/Imperial Palace

Feng-shui design pervades this over-the-top bistro, where a ginormous Buddha floats above an infinity pool. Tableside dim sum service uses traditional carts, or feast on filet mignon with udon noodles or Peking duck. A full bar stocks premium sake labels. Reservations essential, but difficult to score. Dress to impress, as it's a launching pad for Tao (p144) nightclub.

WYNN LAS VEGAS

Reservations (call ☎ 248-3463 or 888-352-3463) and upscale dress are highly recommended.

ALEX
French/Mediterranean $$$

☎ 770-3300; Wynn Las Vegas, 3131 Las Vegas Blvd S; 🕑 6-10pm Thu-Mon; 🚌 Deuce

Award-winning chef Alessandro Stratta stretches his wings at this haute French Riviera restaurant, with wildly successful high-concept dishes such as frog legs with garlic confit and shellfish with pink grapefruit and sea urchin. The pastry chef also triumphs. Reservations are essential, and jackets are suggested for men.

THE BUFFET
Buffet $$

☎ 248-3463; www.wynnlasvegas.com; Wynn Las Vegas, 3131 Las Vegas Blvd S; 🕑 8-10:30am & 11am-3:30pm Mon-Fri, 8am-3:30pm Sat & Sun, 3:30-10pm Sun-Thu, 3:30-10:30pm Fri & Sat; 🚌 Deuce

Wynn's buffet is an uplifting experience, with live-action stations; hot dishes such as tangy barbecue, prime rib and wood-fired pizzas; and some of the freshest fruit, salads and seafood ceviche in town. Delicate desserts and pastries tempt.

DANIEL BOULUD BRASSERIE
French $$

☎ 770-3310; www.danielnyc.com; Wynn Las Vegas, 3131 Las Vegas Blvd S; 🕑 5:30-10:30pm; 🚌 Deuce

All the brasserie classics such as *moules frites* and hanger steak are cooked here, along with more creative carnivorous choices including the signature NY DB Burger stuffed with braised short ribs and topped with black truffles and foie gras on a Parmesan-baked bun. Turn up before 7pm for the three-course prix-fixe menu ($48). Reservations here are recommended.

🍴 TABLEAU
Modern American $$

☎ 248-3463; www.wynnlasvegas.com; Tower Suites, Wynn Las Vegas, 3131 Las Vegas Blvd S; ◷ 8-10:30am & 11:30am-2:30pm Mon-Fri, 8am-2:30pm Sat & Sun, 5:30-10pm daily; 🚌 Deuce

Feel like a VIP inside Wynn's ivory Tower Suites. The biggest payoff at Tableau is at breakfast and brunch, which feature everything from watermelon juice and lemon-ricotta pancakes to tender Kobe beef sandwiches. Skip dinner, though (as it's not great value).

🍴 TERRACE POINT CAFÉ
American $$

☎ 248-3463; www.wynnlasvegas.com; Wynn Las Vegas, 3131 Las Vegas Blvd S; ◷ 24hr; 🚌 Deuce

A refined country-club atmosphere and sunny poolside patio take the casino coffee-shop concept to a whole new level. Well-rehearsed service, enormous portions and whopping prices are sure to knock you out.

DOWNTOWN

🍴 BAY CITY DINER
American/Seafood $

☎ 385-1906; www.goldengatecasino.net; Golden Gate, 1 E Fremont St; ◷ 24hr, shrimp bar & deli 11am-2am; 🚌 Deuce

Cheapo breakfasts, steaks and roast chicken are the draws at this quaint eatery inside Fremont St's most historic hotel (since 1906), where jaunty piano music plays. At the San Francisco Shrimp Bar & Deli, order the best $1.99 shrimp cocktail in town (super-size it for a buck more).

🍴 BINION'S RANCH STEAKHOUSE
Steakhouse $$

☎ 382-1600; www.binions.com; Binion's, 128 E Fremont St; ◷ 5-11pm; 🚌 Deuce

When high-rollin' cowboys finish up in the poker room, they tip back their Stetsons and ride the glass elevator up to this Old Vegas penthouse meatery for stunning 24th-floor views and fine feasts of juicy chops with old-school fixins. Reservations recommended.

🍴 BINION'S SNACK BAR
American $

☎ 382-1600; www.binions.com; Binion's, 128 E Fremont St; ◷ 10am-10pm Sun-Thu, 10am-midnight Fri & Sat; 🚌 Deuce

On the main casino floor, this snack bar's old-fashioned counter plies fresh, never-frozen beef burgers piled high with crackling onions, iceberg lettuce and huge tomato slices. Chat with the sassy old-timers working the grill while wolfing down a slice of cherry pie.

🍴 FLORIDA CAFÉ
Cuban $

☎ 385-3013; www.floridacafecuban .com; Howard Johnson hotel, 1401 Las Vegas Blvd S; 🕐 8am-10pm; 🚌 Deuce; ♿

A hub for Naked City's Cuban community, the Florida has island artworks hanging on the walls and a Cuban chef reigning over the kitchen, cooking up shredded steak, hearty fried pork and

seasoned chicken with yellow rice. *Café con leche,* flan and *batidos* (tropical shakes) are super.

🍴 GROTTO
Italian $$

☎ 385-7111; www.goldennugget .com; Golden Nugget, 129 E Fremont St; 🕐 11:30am-10:30pm Sun-Thu, 11:30am-11:30pm Fri & Sat, pizza oven & bar until 1am; 🚌 Deuce

Let yourself be drawn to the sunny patio beside the Nugget's shark-tank water slide and swimming pool. Gnocchi and osso bucco are the tenor of the old-world menu, but wood oven–fired pizzas and a 200-bottle list of Italian wines are the real stars.

You may think you're eating in Italy at Grotto

🍴 LUV-IT FROZEN CUSTARD
Take-Out $

☎ 384-6452; www.luvitfrozencustard
.com; 505 E Oakey Blvd; 🕑 1-10pm Tue-
Thu, 1-11pm Fri & Sat, also 1-10pm Sun &
Mon May-Aug, closed Dec; 🚌 Deuce; ♿

Open since 1973, Luv-It offers
handmade custard concoctions
that are creamier than ice cream.
Flavors change daily, so you'll be
tempted to go back again, and
again. Try a chocolate-dipped 'Luv
Stick' bar, double-thick milkshake
or superhero-sized sundae. Cash
only.

🍴 MERMAIDS
Fast Food $

☎ 382-5777; 32 E Fremont St; 🕑 24hr;
🚌 Deuce

Hook a strand of Mardi Gras
beads at the door, then weave
your way past the bleary-eyed
slot jockeys to belly up at the
back counter for outrageous
deep-fried Twinkies and Oreos
snowed under by powdered
sugar. So sinfully tasty.

🍴 PULLMAN BAR & GRILLE
Steakhouse $$

☎ 387-1896; www.mainstreetcasino
.com; Main Street Station, 200 N Main
St; 🕑 5-10:30pm Fri & Sat, 5-10pm Sun;
🚌 Deuce

A well-kept secret, the clubby
Pullman features the finest Black
Angus beef and Pacific Rim sea-

food specialties, plus a solid wine
list. Amid gorgeous carved wood
paneling and a fortune's worth
of antiques, the centerpiece is a
1926 Pullman train car, which is
now a cigar lounge where suited-
up patrons quaff an after-dinner
brandy. Reservations are advised
here.

🍴 SECOND STREET GRILL
Steakhouse/Seafood $$

☎ 385-3232; www.fremontcasino.com;
Fremont, 200 E Fremont St; 🕑 5-11pm
Thu-Mon; 🚌 Deuce

At this downtown rococo gem,
which most tourists don't know
about, chef Rachel Bern flies in
seafood fresh from Hawaii. You
can score a 16oz T-bone steak
with all the trimmings for under
20 bucks, or try the regal rack of
lamb.

🍴 TRIPLE GEORGE GRILL
Steakhouse/Seafood $$

☎ 384-2761; www.triplegeorgegrill
.com; 201 N 3rd St; 🕑 11am-10pm Mon-
Fri, 4-11pm Sat; 🚌 Deuce

Showing off swank old-school
San Francisco style, this hideaway
is a haunt of the city's movers
and shakers, attracted not only
by its dry-aged steaks and classic
seafood dishes, but also its Rat
Pack–worthy cocktails and rare
wines, which are also poured next
door at sidebar.

🍴 VIC & ANTHONY'S
Steakhouse/Seafood $$
☎ 386-8399; www.vicandanthonys
.com; Golden Nugget, 129 E Fremont St;
🕑 5-11pm; 🚌 Deuce

Heavy red curtains, a faux
stained-glass ceiling and high-
backed leather chairs comple-
ment the serious atmosphere.
The steakhouse menu covers
the classics: jumbo lump crab
cakes, Maine lobster, grain-fed
Midwestern beef, Beluga caviar
and a divine chocolate fudge
cake. Reservations are recom-
mended.

EAST OF THE STRIP
🍴 AGO
Italian $$
☎ 693-4440; www.hardrockhotel.com;
Hard Rock, 4455 Paradise Rd; 🕑 5:30-
11pm Mon-Thu, 5:30-11:30pm Fri-Sun;
🚌 108, 202; Ⓥ

Backed by Hollywood celeb
Robert DeNiro, chef Agostino
Sciandri's sleek eatery will be hard-

BEST NOSHES OUTSIDE CASINOS
> Rosemary's (p128)
> Firefly (right)
> Origin India (p122)
> Hash House A Go Go (p126)
> Vintner Grill (p129)

pressed to fail. The elegant menu
of northern Italian cuisine includes
signature house-made pastas,
thin-crust pizzas, wild-mushroom
risotto, delicately done seafood
and other meatier fare. Inspired
desserts.

🍴 ENVY
Steakhouse $$
☎ 784-5716; www.envysteakhouse
.com; Renaissance, 3400 Paradise Rd;
🕑 6:30am-2:30pm daily, 5-10pm Sun-
Thu, 5-10:30pm Fri & Sat; Ⓜ Convention
Center

Envy's name is no lie. Near the
convention center, powerbro-
kers recline against high-backed
chairs amid a boldly splashed
color palette. Both steaks and
seafood get high marks, along
with a smart wine list and inven-
tive side dishes like bourbon
creamed corn. At breakfast,
early risers see the likes of
lemony brioche French toast or
gingerbread waffles topped with
cinnamon gelato. Reservations
recommended.

🍴 FIREFLY
Tapas $$
☎ 369-3971; www.fireflylv.com;
Citibank Plaza, 3900 Paradise Rd;
🕑 11:30am-2am Sun-Thu, 11:30am-3am
Fri & Sat; 🚌 108

Firefly is always packed with a
fashionable local crowd, not just

Settle back with a sangria at sizzling Firefly (p121)

for the singles' scene on the late-night patio, but also for the food. Tapas-style dishes are often fusion-spiced, but still shake hands with Spanish tradition, from *patatas bravas* to chorizo clams and vegetarian delights. A backlit bar dispenses the house specialty sangria and infused mojitos. On some nights, hot Latin turntablists spin. Reservations strongly recommended.

🍴 METRO PIZZA
Pizza $

☎ 736-1955; www.metropizza.com; 1395 E Tropicana Ave; ⏰ 11am-10pm Sun-Thu, 11am-11pm Fri & Sat; 🚌 201; 👶

If you don't make it out here to taste Vegas' best thin-crust pie, you can devour a cheesy slice at Metro's outpost in the 24-hour **Ellis Island Casino & Brewery** (☎ 312-5888; 4178 Koval Lane), east of the Strip.

🍴 NOBU
Japanese Fusion $$$

☎ 693-5090; www.hardrockhotel.com; Hard Rock, 4455 Paradise Rd; ⏰ 6-11pm; 🚌 108, 202

Iron Chef Matasuhisa's sequel to his NYC namesake is almost as good as the original. The beats are down-tempo, the setting pure Zen, with bamboo stalks sprouting up around the kitchen. Stick to Nobu's classics, such as black cod with miso. Feeling flush? Try the chef's special *omakase* dinner (from $100). Reservations essential.

🍴 ORIGIN INDIA
Indian $$

☎ 734-6342; www.originindia restaurant.com; 4480 Paradise Rd; ⏰ 11:30am-11:30pm; 🚌 108, 202; Ⓥ

In a chic dining room flecked with gold and outfitted with

high-backed leather chairs, an epic New World and European wine list is only a bonus. What reels in adventurous feasters is the imaginative Indian menu, ranging across the subcontinent from centuries-old royal recipes to modern fusion dishes. The tandoori grills are exceptional. Vegetarians might feel like they've reached nirvana.

🍴 PAYMON'S MEDITERRANEAN CAFÉ
Mediterranean $$

☎ 731-6030; www.paymons.com; 4147 S Maryland Parkway; 🕐 11am-1am Sun-Thu, 11am-3am Fri & Sat; 🚌 109, 202; Ⓥ

A find for vegetarian-friendly Middle Eastern specialties such as baked eggplant with fresh garlic, baba ganoush, bouranni and hummus. Carnivores will savor the succulent rotisserie lamb, baked *kibbe* platter and the hot gyros and kebab sandwiches. The next-door Hookah Lounge (p136) is seductive.

🍴 RED MANGO
Take-Out $

☎ 795-0004; www.redmangousa.com; 4480 Paradise Rd; 🕐 11:30am-1am; 🚌 108, 202

Vanilla and green-tea frozen yogurt with all-natural flavor

toppings such as fresh ruby-red berries are whipped up inside this modish storefront, which looks as if it belongs in fashion-forward Harajuku. Also in **Henderson** (☎ 617-2500; 9480 S Eastern Ave).

🍴 SAN-TOKI KOREAN BBQ & SHABU BAR
Korean $$

☎ 732-8654; www.santokibbq.com; 4480 Paradise Rd; 🕐 5pm-2am; 🚌 108, 202

At this classy Korean barbecue joint, opposite the Hard Rock, raucous groups of friends can gather around the sizzling hot grills and the DIY *shabu* (Asian broth fondue accompanied by spicy and citrus dipping sauces) bar.

🍴 TABLE 34
Modern American $$

☎ 263-0034; 600 E Warm Springs Rd; 🕐 11am-3pm Mon-Fri, 5-10pm Tue-Sat; 🚌 217

Chef Wes Kendrick's seasonal cuisine keeps locals coming back to this airy restaurant south of the airport. Choose from haute modern pastas, pizzas and salads made with heirloom tomatoes and fresh mozzarella, or more substantial mains like chipotle chicken and barbecue-blackened flatiron steak. Top-notch wine bar. Reservations helpful.

Raja Majid & Alana Olevic-Majid
Local taste-bud ticklers, food innovators and owners of Origin India (p122)

Why open a restaurant in a competitive city like Las Vegas? We love
to make restaurants work, to see them grow. **Typical crowd** About 50/50,
locals and tourists. **The biggest challenge?** Changing people's perceptions
of Indian food in America. What we are trying to do is to give a taste of real
Indian flavors, to introduce evolved Indian food that's also fresh, organic
and healthy. Our chef specializes in Ayurvedic cooking. **What don't people
know about Indian cuisine?** The spices are so strong, people don't know
what wine they should drink, or if they should even drink wine. But they
should. **What don't people know about Las Vegas?** How little the Strip is,
and how big everything else is. **Best experiences for out-of-town visitors**
Go see the shows (p144) – and the Grand Canyon (p156), too.

WEST OF THE STRIP

🍽 ALIZÉ

French $$$

☎ 951-7000; www.alizelv.com; 56th fl, Palms, 4321 W Flamingo Rd; ⏱ 5:30-10pm Sun-Thu, 5:30-11pm Fri & Sat; 🚌 202

Las Vegas chef André Rochat's top-drawer gourmet room is named after a gentle Mediterranean trade wind. Enjoyed by nearly every table, the panoramic floor-to-ceiling views of the glittering Strip are even more stunning than the haute French cuisine. A wine-bottle tower dominates the room. Reservations here are essential. Dress to the nines.

🍽 ARTEM (ELISEEVSKY)

Russian $$

☎ 247-8766; www.russianvegas.com; 4825 W Flamingo Rd; ⏱ 5pm-1am Tue-Sun; 🚌 202

At this woodsy cabin that resembles a wintery *Doctor Zhivago* set, Russian singers belt it out on weekends. Cirque du Soleil performers often come here, dining with a fun-loving crowd on Slavic salads, borsch soup and blini with beautiful dollops of black caviar.

🍽 CARNIVAL WORLD & VILLAGE SEAFOOD BUFFETS

Buffet $$

☎ 777-7777; www.riolasvegas.com; Rio, 3700 W Flamingo Rd; ⏱ Carnival World 7am-10pm Mon-Fri, 7:30am-10pm Sat & Sun, Village Seafood 4-10pm Sun-Thu, 4-11pm Fri & Sat; 🚌 free Strip shuttle

Some say Carnival World is Vegas' best all-around buffet, with wok-fried dishes, taco bars, fresh seafood and handmade gelato. Pricier Village Seafood is for those who can't get enough snow crab legs, lobster tails and fresh-shucked oysters, plus salads and house-made breads.

🍽 CHINATOWN PLAZA

Pan-Asian $

☎ 221-8448; www.lvchinatown.com; 4215 Spring Mountain Rd; ⏱ daily, hours vary; 🚌 203

Lively Asian restaurants anchor around the Chinese gate on Spring Mountain Rd in Chinatown, where you'll also find plenty of Hong Kong barbecue houses, Vietnamese pho shops, Japanese sushi bars and pan-Asian bubble-tea dispensaries.

🍽 CUPCAKERY

Take-Out $

☎ 207-2253; www.thecupcakery.com; 9680 S Eastern Ave; ⏱ 8am-6pm Mon-Wed, 8am-8pm Thu-Fri, 10am-8pm Sat, noon-6pm Sun; 🚌 110

Like a *Wizard of Oz* fantasyland, this maniacally cute storefront sells fresh-baked cupcakes in a Wonka-esque variety of flavors, from chocolate passion to coconut bliss. Sadly, the exquisite packaging is an eco-unfriendly waste.

🍽 GARDUÑO'S
Southwestern $$

☎ 942-7777; www.palms.com; Palms, 4321 W Flamingo Rd; ⏰ 11am-9:30pm Mon, 11am-10pm Tue-Thu, 11am-11pm Fri & Sat, 10:30am-3pm & 4-10pm Sun; 🚌 202

From Albuquerque's famed restaurant, the *tradicional* menu of New Mexican fare features such authentic tastes as handmade pork tamales and blue-corn enchiladas filled with chicken and cheese and doused with green and red chili sauces. Belly up to the Blue Agave oyster and chili bar for shooters and coconut margaritas.

🍽 GOLDEN STEER
Steakhouse $$

☎ 384-4470; www.goldensteerlv .com; 308 W Sahara Ave; ⏰ 5-11pm; 🚌 Deuce

It's not the best steak in town. So why are you eating at this fabulously retro steakhouse with the steer's head out front? It's the same place where the Rat Pack and Elvis once dined. You're here to soak up the Old Vegas vibes.

> ### BEST BREAKFAST BETS
> > Envy (Renaissance; p121)
> > Hash House A Go Go (below)
> > Il Fornaio (New York–New York; p110)
> > Le Village Buffet (Paris Las Vegas; p113)
> > Tableau (Wynn Las Vegas; p118)

🍽 HASH HOUSE A GO GO
American $$

☎ 804-4646; www.hashhouseagogo .com; 6800 W Sahara Ave, east of S Rainbow Blvd; ⏰ 7:30am-2:30pm daily, 5-10pm Mon-Sat; 🚌 204; V ♿

Before heading to Red Rock Canyon (p160), fill up on this So-Cal import's famed 'twisted farm food,' which has to be seen to be believed. The pancakes are as big as tractor tires and the farm-egg scrambles and huge hashes could knock over a cow. Meatloaf, pot pies, chicken 'n' biscuits and wild-boar sloppy joes are what's for dinner.

🍽 IN-N-OUT BURGER
Fast Food $

☎ 800-786-1000; www.in-n-out.com; 4888 Dean Martin Dr; ⏰ 10:30am-1am Sun-Thu, 10:30am-1:30am Fri & Sat; 🚌 202; ♿

At California's famous In-N-Out, where the beef patties are never frozen and the potatoes are hand-diced daily, there's a secret menu. Ask for your burger 'animal style' (with mustard, an onion-grilled bun and extra-special sauce).

🍴 LOUIE'S FISH CAMP
Cajun/Creole $$

☎ 463-3000; www.louieslasvegas.com; Town Square mall, 6605 Las Vegas Blvd S; ⏱ 11am-11pm; 🚌 Deuce

Straight from the South Carolina low country, island-style Louie's piles plates high with flash-fried alligator, jumbo crab-and-lobster cakes and other down-home goodness, then pours stiff bourbons and mint juleps at the bar. Show up for live bands on Thursday, Friday and Saturday nights. Around the corner, **Louie's** (☎ 202-2400; ⏱ 5:30-10pm) fine-dining restaurant does a tempting three-course Sunday brunch ($35; available from 11am to 2:30pm).

🍴 N9NE
Steakhouse/Seafood $$$

☎ 933-9900; www.n9nesteakhouse .com; Palms, 4321 W Flamingo Rd; ⏱ 5:30-10:30pm Sun-Thu, 5:30-11:30pm Fri & Sat; 🚌 202

The Palms' sizzling steakhouse is a fave spot to sometimes spy on Hollywood celebs. A dramatically lit room centers on the champagne caviar bar, while at tables and booths the Chicago-style aged steaks and chops keep on coming, along with everything else from oysters Rockefeller to

Pacific-caught sashimi. Reservations essential.

🍴 NORA'S WINE BAR & OSTERIA
Italian $$

☎ 940-6672; www.noraswinebar.com; 1031 S Rampart Blvd; ⏱ 11am-10pm Sun-Thu, 11am-11pm Fri & Sat; 🚌 206

Across the street from chichi Boca Park Fashion Village (p92), Nora's is a polished spot for *ciccheti* (small bites) such as Parmesan-stuffed dates or eggplant cakes, and more substantial meals like Sicilian breaded pork tenderloin with roasted tomatoes. At the lively wine bar, five-dozen wines are kept fresh and chilled by a high-tech wine-dispensing system. Reservations are recommended here.

🍴 PING PANG PONG
Chinese $$

☎ 367-7111; www.goldcoastcasino .com; Gold Coast, 4000 W Flamingo Rd; ⏱ 10am-3pm & 5pm-3am; 🚌 202

Asian tourists vote with their feet, and it's always crowded here. Designed by chef Kevin Wu, a wok-tossed menu ranges across the regions of China, from Beijing seafood stew to Shanghai noodles. At lunchtime the dim sum cart rolls around. Service is fast and furious at the less-expensive **Noodle Exchange** (⏱ 3pm-midnight).

ROSEMARY'S
Modern American $$

☎ 869-2251; www.rosemarysrestaurant
.com; 8125 W Sahara Ave, west of S Buffalo
Dr; ⏰ 11:30am-2:30pm Mon-Fri, 5:30-
10:30pm daily; 🚌 204

Words almost fail to describe the
epicurean ecstasy you'll encounter
here. Yes, it's in a strip mall, and
it's a long drive from the Strip. But
once you bite into such divine of-
ferings as Texas barbecue shrimp
with Maytag blue-cheese slaw
or grilled pork chops with Creole
mustard sauce, you'll forget about
all that. Wine and beer pairings are
sublime. Reservations essential.

SALT LICK BBQ
Barbecue $$

☎ 797-7535; www.redrocklasvegas
.com; Red Rock Casino Resort Spa, 11011
W Charleston Blvd at I-215; ⏰ 4-9pm
Mon-Fri, 2-9pm Sat & Sun; 🚌 206

Straight from the Lone Star State,
this authentic 'cue joint gets a
big thumbs-up. After a hard day's
play on the Red Rock range, chow
down here on slow-smoked pork
ribs, succulent beef brisket,
southern-style pulled pork and
filling sides such as smoked
mac 'n' cheese and cool coleslaw.
Take-out available. Yee-haw!

Delight in sushi and sake at Social House (p116)

🍴 VEGGIE DELIGHT
Vegetarian $

☎ 310-6565; 3504 Wynn Rd; ⏰ 11am-8pm; 🚌 203; Ⓥ

Just south of Chinatown's main drag, this peaceful, Buddhist-owned vegetarian (and vegan, upon request) restaurant cooks Vietnamese-style soups, crispy baguette sandwiches and summer rolls. A healthy menu of Chinese herbal tonics is color-coded to your chakras.

🍴 VINTNER GRILL
Mediterranean $$

☎ 214-5590; www.vglasvegas.com; 10100 W Charleston Blvd, off Indigo Dr; ⏰ 11am-10pm Sun-Thu, 11am-11pm Fri & Sat

Inside an office park, this surprisingly elegant space lures romantics to its enchanting canopied patio, where white lights twinkle over white sofas. Bite into wood oven–fired flatbreads, panini, seafood and soups at lunch. At dinner, classics such as veal London broil and lamb osso bucco show off continental touches. Decadent desserts are by Vosges Haut-Chocolat. Reservations are recommended here.

AFTER HOURS
Late-night dining hot spots and 'graveyard' special meal deals come and go, but **Ellis Island Casino & Brewery** (☎ 733-8901; www.ellisislandcasino.com; 4178 Koval Lane) is hard to beat, offering a full 10oz steak dinner ($6.99) around-the-clock. Other good late-night dining bets include **SushiSamba** (p112), **Social House** (p116), **Firefly** (p121), **Paymon's Mediterranean Café** (p123), **San-Toki Korean BBQ & Shabu Bar** (p123), **Ping Pang Pong** (p127) and **In-N-Out Burger** (p126).

⭐ PLAY

The Strip is the obvious all-hours hot spot. Catch a stage show before midnight, groove to a DJ till dawn, then unwind at a sultry spa after noon. This cow town also attracts more than its share of headliners, including celebrity entertainers you may have thought were already dead – whoops!

You can go broke seeing and doing all there is to see and do on the Strip, or be entertained for zero money at fun, free-for-all spectacles like the Bellagio's dancing fountains. Las Vegans let loose at hipster haunts on the edges of downtown, student- and gay-friendly hangouts east of the Strip, strip clubs in industrial areas west of I-15, and neighborhood bars and casinos in the 'burbs.

Free alternative tabloids *Las Vegas Weekly* (www.lasvegasweekly.com) and *Las Vegas CityLife* (www.lvcitylife.com) hit the streets on Thursday and, when combined with the 'Neon' section of the *Las Vegas Review-Journal* on Friday, offer comprehensive arts, entertainment and events listings. So do free, encyclopedic tourist mags such as *What's On* and *Las Vegas Magazine + Showbiz Weekly*.

THAT'S THE TICKET!

Ticketmaster (☎ 474-4000; www.ticketmaster.com) Tickets for major sporting events, headliner concerts and more.
Tix 4 Tonight (☎ 877-849-4868; www.tix4tonight.com) Center Strip (Fashion Show, 3200 Las Vegas Blvd S; ☼ 10am-8pm); downtown (Four Queens, 202 E Fremont St; ☼ 10am-8pm); North Strip (2955 Las Vegas Blvd S; ☼ 10am-8pm); South Strip (Hawaiian Marketplace, 3743 Las Vegas Blvd S; ☼ 10am-8pm) Also sells same-day discount tickets in front of the giant Coca-Cola bottle, just north of the MGM Grand.

Top left Lose your Zen on the dance floor at Tao (p144) **Bottom left** Dazzle and be dazzled on the patio of Pure (p144)

LAS VEGAS CALENDAR

Las Vegas is a nonstop party 24/7/365. Holidays (p192) are taken to the max, with New Year's Eve along the Strip seeing the biggest crush of humanity this side of Times Sq. Major sports events (p149) also pack the city like a full house. Contact the **Las Vegas Convention & Visitors Authority** (LVCVA; ☎ 892-0711, 877-847-4858; www.visitlasvegas.com; 3150 Paradise Rd; ✿ office 8am-5pm, toll-free hotline 6am-9pm) for current events info.

March
Vegas High Rollers (www.lvscooterrally.com) Retro bowling and pinball nights, poker tournaments, ska bands and dances, and fab happy hours jazz up this scooter rally.

April
UNLVino (www.unlvino.com) Nonprofit wine-tasting extravaganza brings together oenophiles and more than 350 winemakers for tastings and an art-and-wine auction.
Viva Las Vegas (www.vivalasvegas.net) Ultimate rockabilly weekend comes alive with a tiki pool party, jive-dancing classes, a va-va-va-voom burlesque competition and souped-up classic car show.

May
Helldorado Days (www.elkshelldorado.com) Dating back to the 1930s, this historic hoedown features rodeo events, barbecues, country fiddlers and an Old West frontier town by the Fremont Street Experience.

June & July
CineVegas (www.cinevegas.com) Prestigious nine-day film festival showcases indie flicks, first-time directors and some major Hollywood faces at the Palms (p55).

 BARS

Most of Sin City's watering holes are smoke-filled, and antismoking bans are viewed with heartfelt disdain. Many bars stay open until 2am or even around-the-clock. Happy hours are usually 4pm till 7pm, with 'graveyard' happy hours after midnight.

 BAR AT TIMES SQUARE
☎ 740-6969; www.nynyhotelcasino.com; Greenwich Village, New York–New York, 3790 Las Vegas Blvd S; cover $10; ✿ 10am-2am Mon-Wed, 10am-3am Thu & Sun, 10am-4am Fri & Sat (live music 3-7pm Thu-Sun & 8pm-2:30am daily); Ⓜ MGM Grand
Baby boomers will dig the sing-along vibe at this dueling piano

World Series of Poker (www.worldseriesofpoker.com) High-stakes gamblers, casino employees and celebrities match wits in over 40 tournaments. Free public viewing.

August
Def Con (www.defcon.org) The nation's biggest conclave of underground computer hackers takes place over a long, heavily caffeinated weekend.

September
Las Vegas BikeFest (www.lasvegasbikefest.com) This bike rally brings hogs and heifers and Harley-riding poker players roaring into town, with barbecues and bikinis part of the debauchery.

October
Vegoose (www.vegoose.com) Over Halloween weekend, this zany music-and-arts festival has live indie bands, interactive performance art and lotsa costumed partying.

November
Aviation Nation (www.aviationnation.org) At Nellis Air Force Base, this is the nation's most famous military and civilian air show, during which the Thunderbirds, an aerial demonstration team, often zooms in.

December
Wrangler National Finals Rodeo (www.nfrexperience.com) This hugely popular 10-day event features professional rodeo cowboys competing in a half-dozen adrenaline-driven events, including steer wrestling and bull riding.

bar. Show up early or risk waiting outside in Greenwich Village, where latecomers strain to catch a glimpse of the drunken festivities inside.

 BEAUTY BAR
☎ 598-1965; www.beautybar.com; 517 E Fremont St; cover free-$10; 🕐 usually 9:30pm-late Sat-Thu, 5pm-late Fri; 🚌 Deuce

Swill a cocktail, watch the weekly manicure demonstrations or just chill inside the salvaged innards of a 1950s New Jersey beauty salon. DJs and live bands rotate nightly here, spinning tiki lounge tones, '80s garage rock, punk, funk and soul. Make sure you wear your coolest vintage threads.

⭐ CARNAVAL COURT

☎ 369-5000; www.harrahslasvegas
.com; outside Harrah's, 3475 Las Vegas
Blvd S; 🕑 noon-2am; Ⓜ Harrah's/
Imperial Palace

Flair bartenders juggle fire for
raucous crowds for whom spring
break never ended. Live pop and
rock cover bands tear up the stage
at night, but all eyes are on the hot
bods at the bar. Party on, dudes.

⭐ DOWNTOWN COCKTAIL ROOM

☎ 880-3696; www.downtownlv.net;
111 Las Vegas Blvd S; cover free–$20;
🕑 4pm-late Mon-Fri, 7pm-late Sat &
Sun; 🚌 Deuce

With a retro cocktail list you must
take seriously, this speakeasy with
sateen pillows and suede-covered
couches feels decades removed
from the old-school carpet joints
on Fremont St. In true Prohibition-
era style, the entrance is disguised.

⭐ FIRESIDE LOUNGE

☎ 735-4177; www.peppermilllasvegas
.com; Peppermill, 2985 Las Vegas Blvd S;
🕑 24hr; 🚌 Deuce

Don't be blinded by the outlandish
rainbow-colored neon lights: the
Strip's most spellbinding hideaway
awaits inside this retro coffee shop.
Courting couples adore the sunken
fire pit, cozy blue-velvet nooks and
faux tropical foliage. Sip a Scorpion.

DRINKS WITH VIP VIEWS

> Fontana Bar (Bellagio;
  below)
> Ghostbar (Palms; p153)
> Moon (Palms; p143)
> Mix (THEhotel at Mandalay Bay;
  p136)
> Romance at Top of the World
  (Stratosphere; p137)

⭐ FONTANA BAR

🕑 693-7111; www.bellagio.com; Bella-
gio, 3600 Las Vegas Blvd S; 🕑 5pm-1am
Sun-Thu, 5pm-2am Fri-Sat; Ⓜ Bally's/
Paris

An older, well-heeled crowd un-
winds at this haute casino lounge
that has live jazz and a lakeview
patio safely removed from the hoi
polloi on the Strip. It's perfect for
watching the Bellagio's dancing-
fountain shows.

⭐ FREEZONE

☎ 794-2300; www.freezonelv.com;
610 E Naples Dr, off Paradise Rd; 🕑 24hr;
🚌 108

Every night is a party at this gay
dive bar. Tuesday is ladies' night
with go-go girls, Thursday is boyz'
night with go-go boys, Friday
and Saturday nights feature the
'Queens of Las Vegas' drag
cabaret, and Sunday and Monday
are for free pool and no-wait
karaoke.

⭐ GOLD DIGGERS

☎ 385-7111; www.goldennugget
.com; Golden Nugget, 129 E Fremont St;
🕑 7pm-late Tue-Sun; 🚌 Deuce

If you're tired of the Strip's velvet ropes and just want a place to get fully loaded and boogie, hit the Nugget's bumpin' upstairs bar and dance floor. An open-air patio overhanging the Fremont Street Experience is made for both voyeurs and exhibitionists.

⭐ GOODTIMES

☎ 736-9494; www.goodtimeslv.com;
1775 E Tropicana Ave; 🕑 24hr; 🚌 201

A gay men's club where conversation rules, there's also a steel dance floor, video poker, pool

tables and a legendary Monday liquor bust (all-you-can-drink happy hour) from 11pm to 4am. It's built next door to the Liberace Museum (p79). A coincidence? We think not.

⭐ GRIFFIN

☎ 382-0577; 511 E Fremont St; cover
free-$10; 🕑 5pm-2am Mon-Sat, 9pm-
2am Sun; 🚌 Deuce

Escape from the casinos' clutch and imbibe at this indie joint, a short walk along the dark side of Fremont St. Crackling fireplaces, leather booths and an almost unbearably cool jukebox make it popular with hipster sweethearts and rebels alike.

Choose your own wicked concoction at Carnaval Court

SPECIALTY DRINKS

Double Helix (Shoppes at Palazzo; p94) A robust wine list from around the world is poured at a stand-and-pose circular bar. There are customized flights and a smart sommelier.

Isla Tequila Bar (Isla Mexican Kitchen; p115) Let the 'tequila goddess' guide you through the wonderland of premium agave elixirs.

Nine Fine Irishmen (New York–New York; p53) Stout Irish beers, rare whiskies and other spirits; traditional music and Celtic rock; and Brooklyn Bridge views.

Pour 24 (New York–New York; p53) Next to the pedestrian skybridge, North American microbrews on draft or in bottles are popped open around-the-clock.

Red Square (Mandalay Bay; p50) A headless Lenin invites you behind the blood-red curtains for a tipple of vodka and caviar dished up on a solid ice bar. For pirates' grog, rumjungle is next door.

⭐ HOFBRÄUHAUS

☎ 853-2337; www.hofbrauhauslas vegas.com; 4510 Paradise Rd; 🕑 11am-11pm Sun-Thu, 11am-midnight Fri & Sat; 🚍 108, 202

A fawning replica of the original in Munich, this $12-million beer hall and garden celebrates Oktoberfest all year with premium imported suds, big Bavarian pretzels, fair fräuleins, trademark *gemütlichkeit* (congeniality) and nightly oom-pah-pah bands direct from Germany.

⭐ HOOKAH LOUNGE

☎ 731-6030; www.hookahlounge .com; 4147 S Maryland Parkway; 🕑 5pm-1am Mon-Thu, 5pm-3am Fri & Sat; 🚍 109, 202

Next to Paymon's Mediterranean Café (p123), you can recline languorously with a water pipe stuffed with one of 20 premium flavored Egyptian tobaccos. Exotic fig-flavored cocktails are pricier than the off-Strip norm, but for ambience worthy of a pasha, why not?

⭐ MIX

☎ 632-9500; www.mandalaybay.com; 64th fl, THEhotel at Mandalay Bay, 3950 Las Vegas Blvd S; cover after 10pm $25; 🕑 5pm-2am Sun-Thu, 5pm-4am Fri & Sat; 🚍 Deuce

Arrive at around sunset for a free glass elevator ride up to this sky-high restaurant lounge with some of Las Vegas' most breathtaking views – and that's even before you glimpse the wall-to-wall leather seating and the champagne bar. Go hobnobbing on the vertiginous outdoor patio.

⭐ NAPOLEON'S

☎ 946-7000; www.parislasvegas.com; Le Boulevard, Paris Las Vegas, 3655 Las Vegas Blvd S; ☣ 4pm-2am; Ⓜ Bally's/Paris

Whisk yourself off to a never-neverland of 19th-century France, with a mosaic floor and overstuffed sofas that are as luxurious as the menu of 100 types of bubbly, including vintage Dom Perignon – soar on a 'champagne flight.'

⭐ ROMANCE AT TOP OF THE WORLD

☎ 380-7711; www.topoftheworldlv .com; 107th fl, Stratosphere Tower, 2000 Las Vegas Blvd S; elevator ride $14; ☣ 4pm-1am Sun-Thu, 4pm-2am Fri & Sat; Ⓜ Sahara

There's no place to get any higher in Vegas without the approval of an air-traffic controller. From Wednesday through Saturday evenings, smooth jazz accompanies the 'elevated' martinis swilled by a moneyed crowd of cocktail-hour couples. Chic dress code.

⭐ TRADER VIC'S

☎ 405-4700; www.tradervicslv.com; Miracle Mile Shops, 3663 Las Vegas Blvd S; ☣ restaurant & bar 11:30am-midnight Mon-Thu, 11am-midnight Fri-Sun, lounge 9pm-4am Mon & Thu-Sat; Ⓜ Bally's/Paris

The legendary Polynesian tiki bar that first formulated the mai tai

cocktail in San Francisco in the 1930s has been reinvented on the Strip, right down to the bamboo walls and zebra-print furnishings. Head upstairs to the ultra lounge, where palm trees wave over a Strip-view patio and DJs mix ear-tickling electronica.

⭐ TRIPLE 7

☎ 387-1896; www.mainstreetcasino .com; Main Street Station, 200 N Main St; ☣ 24hr; 🚌 Deuce

Sports fans and a crusty crowd of local gamblers flock to this gargantuan brewpub for Monday Night Football, happy hour and graveyard specials. Five micro-brews on tap (including specialty fruit beers) and cheap pub grub sate the punters. Don't expect snappy service, though.

⭐ CINEMAS

Check **Fandango** (☎ 800-326-3264; www.fandango.com) for show times and tickets.

⭐ BRENDEN THEATRES & IMAX

☎ 507-4849; www.brendentheatres .com; Palms, 4321 W Flamingo Rd; adult/concession $10/6.50, IMAX $14/11; 🚌 202; ♿

Home to the CineVegas film festival (see the boxed text, p132) and showing new Hollywood releases, the swankest off-Strip movieplex is fitted with IMAX and Lucasfilm THX digital sound, plus rocker-chair stadium seating for superior sight lines.

⭐ REGAL VILLAGE SQUARE 18

☎ 221-2283; 9400 W Sahara Ave at S Fort Apache Rd; adult/concession $10/6.50; 🚌 204; ♿

Las Vegas doesn't really have any arthouse cinemas, but this multiplex way out west of the Strip usually has a couple of interesting indie flicks up on the marquee.

⭐ WEST WIND LAS VEGAS DRIVE-IN

☎ 646-3565; 4150 W Carey Ave, east of N Rancho Dr; admission per adult/child $6.25/1; ⏰ gates open 1hr before show time; ♿

One of Nevada's last remaining drive-ins, this old-fashioned place screens up to five double features daily. Bring your buddies, grab some popcorn and put your feet up on the dashboard – ah, heaven.

⭐ COMEDY & MAGIC

Big-name comedians frequently headline at the Flamingo (p46), Golden Nugget (p47), Mandalay Bay (see the boxed text, p151) and MGM Grand (see the boxed text, p151). In November, the **Comedy Festival** (www.thecomedyfestival.com) brings Hollywood funny faces to Caesars Palace.

⭐ COMEDY STOP

☎ 739-2714; www.comedystop.com; Tropicana, 3801 Las Vegas Blvd S; tickets incl 1 drink $22; ⏰ 8pm (nonsmoking) & 10:30pm (smoking); Ⓜ MGM Grand

Be sure to check out the A-list funny men and women cracking up the crowd at the Trop. You can find them in the mezzanine-level cabaret at this Atlantic City export.

⭐ THE IMPROV

☎ 369-5223; www.improv.com; Harrah's, 3475 Las Vegas Blvd S; tickets $29; ⏰ 8:30pm & 10:30pm Tue-Sun; Ⓜ Harrah's/Imperial Palace

The Vegas franchise of this NYC-based chain has that signature Big Apple brick backdrop. The spotlight is on many of the touring stand-up headliners of the moment, often polished by recent late-night TV appearances.

⭐ LANCE BURTON: MASTER MAGICIAN

☎ 730-7160, 877-386-8224; www.lanceburton.com; Monte Carlo, 3770 Las Vegas Blvd S; tickets $67-73; ⏰ 7pm Tue-Sat, 10pm Tue & Sat; 🚌 Deuce; ♿

There are lots of magicians in Vegas, but few have lasted so long. Lance differs from the rest of the pack of magicians by emphasizing sleight-of-hand tricks and other close-up magic. Grand illusions include a signature 'flying' white Corvette.

⭐ MAC KING

☎ 369-5222; www.mackingshow .com; Harrah's, 3475 Las Vegas Blvd S; tickets $25; 🕑 1pm & 3pm Tue-Sat; Ⓜ Harrah's/Imperial Palace; ♿ Redheaded Mac has the front-running afternoon magic and comedy show in town, with lots of PG-13 laughs and sleight-of-hand thrown in. He really rides the crazy train with his bag of tricks, which includes baiting a live goldfish with a Fig Newton cookie.

⭐ PENN & TELLER

☎ 777-7776; www.pennandteller.com; Rio, 3700 W Flamingo Rd; tickets $75-85; 🕑 9pm Wed-Sun; 🚌 free Strip shuttle This intellectual odd couple (one talks, the other doesn't) has been creating and destroying illusions for over two decades, with dry wit, peppery profanity and some amazing stunts such as catching bullets in their teeth. The gimmick is that they actually explain some (but not all) of their tricks to the audience.

⭐ LIVE MUSIC

Don't miss the crazy, crankin' indie-music fest Vegoose (see the boxed text, p132). For Vegas' famous Elvis impersonator shows,

---

LAS VEGAS IDOL

Dino's (☎ 382-3894; 1516 Las Vegas Blvd S; 🚌 Deuce) At this downtown dive bar favored by artists, hipsters and indie types, 'no bullshit' karaoke takes over on Thursday, Friday and Saturday nights (with Jägerbombs!).
Harrah's Piano Bar (near Carnaval Court; p134) It's TJ's All-Star Karaoke Party pretty much every night, with plasma screens, impressionists and stand-up comedy acts.
House of Blues (p140) 'Rock Star Karaoke' is the place to be on Monday nights. Hop on stage with the live band (they sing back-up) and everyone's your groupie.
Karaoke Club (Imperial Palace; p66) Choose from over 15,000 songs and have your performance immortalized on DVD any night of the week. If you're lucky, you'll perform even better than the IP's 'dealertainers' (p78).

---

surf to www.thedreamking.com or www.spiritoftheking.com.

⭐ BUNKHOUSE SALOON

☎ 384-4536; www.bunkhouselv.com; 124 S 11th St; 🕑 24hr; 🚌 107 As you might have guessed, it's got a cowboy theme, with Old West art and saddles lying about. But the real draws are live local bands, anything from rockabilly to rock to reggae, along with indie film and stand-up comedy nights.

⭐ DOUBLE DOWN SALOON

☎ 791-5775; www.doubledownsaloon
.com; 4640 Paradise Rd, enter off Swenson St; ⏱ 24hr; 🚌 108

You just gotta love a punk bar
where the tangy, blood-red house
drink is named 'Ass Juice.' There's
never a cover charge, and the
drinks (try the bacon martini) are
cash only. Monday is the Bargain
DJ Collective night, and there are
lotsa lunatic-fringe bands other
nights. Play pool, pinball, Aster-
oids or the legendary jukebox.

⭐ HOUSE OF BLUES

☎ 632-7600; www.hob.com; Mandalay
Bay, 3950 Las Vegas Blvd S; most tickets
$15-100; ⏱ hours vary; 🚌 Deuce

Blues is the tip of the hog at this
Mississippi Delta juke joint, where
kickin' acts range from living legends to alt-rockers. Seating is
limited, so show up early. Sight lines
are good, and the tattoo studio is
packed with twentysomethings.

⭐ THE JOINT

☎ 693-5066; www.hardrockhotel.com;
Hard Rock, 4455 Paradise Rd; most tickets
$35-175; ⏱ hours vary; 🚌 108, 202

Concerts at this intimate venue
feel like private shows, even when
Coldplay or the Beastie Boys are in
town. It's a beacon for rock 'n' roll
superstars. Most shows here are
standing-room only, with reserv-
able VIP balcony seats upstairs.

⭐ THE PEARL

☎ 944-3200; www.palms.com; Palms,
4321 W Flamingo Rd; most tickets
$25-150; ⏱ hours vary; 🚌 202

A beacon for rock bands, the Palms'
concert hall has a sophisticated
sound system and on-site recording
studio. Modern rock acts like Gwen
Stefani and Morrissey have burned
up the stage, with most seats only
120ft or less away from the stars.

⭐ SAND DOLLAR BLUES LOUNGE

☎ 871-6651; www.sanddollarblues
.com; 3355 Spring Mountain Rd, off Polaris
Ave; cover Wed-Sat $5; ⏱ 24hr; 🚌 203

When you're on your last dime,
drive to this nautical-themed dive.
A few doors down from a Harley re-
pair shop, this unpretentious club is
the only one in town featuring live
blues almost nightly (except Mon-
days) after 10pm. It's smoky, casual
and draws a tough local crowd.

⭐ THEATER BALLROOM

☎ 385-7111, 866-946-5336; www
.goldennugget.com; Golden Nugget, 129
E Fremont St; ⏱ hours vary; 🚌 Deuce

Crooners like Tony Bennett fill the
Nugget's gorgeous 2nd-floor concert hall. Headliners have only short
engagements here, but make for
a sophisticated evening. No-cover
acts like the Frankie Moreno Band
heat up the Rush Lounge downstairs, just off the casino floor.

Andrea Tiede
RawVegas.tv host, runway model, comedic actress and red-carpet guerrilla journalist

How you keep cool on the red carpet Holding onto my own personality. **Best part of your job** Every weekend I have a great club to go to with VIP treatment. We live in a celebrity-obsessed nation, so being a part of it, it's quite the experience. Living in Sin City is the icing on the cake. **What's the upside of living here, not LA or NYC?** What people don't realize is, there's a lot more to do than just the Strip. There's Mt Charleston, for skiing and snowboarding, and Lake Mead (p158), if you like to wakeboard. Vegas has a lot to offer if you're into extreme or outdoor sports. **Best time of year to visit Vegas** Summer is a love/hate proposition. In summer, you'll see so many beautiful people – lots of boobs, testosterone and steroids. And that's comical, how people come here and get these porn-star alter egos. Summer pool parties just top it off. **Three words to describe Las Vegas** Raw, sultry, sophisticated.

NIGHTCLUBS

Ladies sometimes get in free before midnight, especially on weeknights. Call ahead for bottle-service reservations (minimum $200 per foursome). Surf to www.vegas.com for sneak peeks, event calendars and front-of-the-line and VIP passes.

☆ THE BANK
☎ 693-8300; www.lightgroup.com; Bellagio, 3600 Las Vegas Blvd S; cover $50; ⏱ 10:30pm-4am Thu-Sun; Ⓜ Bally's/Paris

A celeb hangout since the day it opened, the posh reincarnation of Light nightclub is cloaked in royal-purple curtains and chandeliers. Lavish multitiered VIP booths are layered around a glass-enclosed dance floor where high-NRG pop and hip hop mixes dominate. Upscale dress code.

☆ BODY ENGLISH
☎ 693-4000; www.bodyenglish.com; Hard Rock, 4455 Paradise Rd; cover $20-40; ⏱ 10pm-4am Wed & Fri-Sun; 🚌 108, 202

Stylin' like a rock star, this chic nightclub has famous faces hanging out in VIP rooms and leather booths, while hoi-polloi masses bump to hip hop, house and rock tunes below a crystal chandelier. Saucy 'Sunday School' and Wednesday's 'Godskitchen' are big nights here. Dress code is 'denim to diamonds.'

☆ FOUNDATION ROOM
☎ 632-7631; www.hob.com; 43rd fl, Mandalay Bay, 3950 Las Vegas Blvd S; ⏱ by invitation only; 🚌 Deuce

House of Blues' (p140) exclusive club atop M-Bay hosts after-show parties in a luxurious lounge with gothic and Indian-temple decor. Celebs such as Andre Agassi hold court, while DJs and special events like Monday's **Godspeed** (www.myspace.com/godspeedlasvegas) enliven the vibe. Call or email (lvviprelations@hob.com) to get on the guest list.

☆ GIPSY
☎ 731-1919; www.gipsylv.net; 4605 S Paradise Rd; cover $5-10; ⏱ 10pm-late; 🚌 108

Nowadays it's looking tattered, and it's no longer the premier gay dance club in town, but there's always a mixed crowd at this giant thumpa-thumpa nightclub, a cocktail shaker's throw south of the Hard Rock. Ladies-only nights, too.

☆ JET
☎ 693-8300; http://jetlv.com; Mirage, 3400 Las Vegas Blvd S; cover $30-50; ⏱ 10:30pm-4am Thu-Sat & Mon; 🚌 Deuce

A sophisticated tri-environment club, Jet once broke the sound barrier in racing to the creamy top of the Strip's nightlife scene. Follow the flickering candles and a staircase made for strutting onto the throbbing dance floor, or sidle into more intimate lounges where the beats run to deep house and hip hop. Stylish attire required.

⭐ KRÄVE

☎ 836-0830; www.kravelasvegas .com; Miracle Mile Shops, 3663 Las Vegas Blvd S, enter off Harmon Ave; cover $20; ⏰ 11pm-late Tue-Sun; Ⓜ Bally's/Paris

The Strip's only gay club is a glam place packed wall-to-wall with hard bodies, plush booth seating, VIP cabañas and even 'airotic' flyboys. The side lounge has salsa, goth and Candybar girls-only nights. Saturday's after-hours party revs up after 4am.

⭐ MOON

☎ 942-6832; http://moon-lasvegas .n9negroup.com; 53rd fl, Fantasy Tower, Palms, 4321 W Flamingo Rd; cover $40; ⏰ 10pm-4am Tue & Thu-Sun; 🚌 202

A short glass-and-mirror elevator ride away from the **Playboy Club** (☎ 942-6832; 52nd fl, Fantasy Tower; cover $20, incl Moon nightclub $40; ⏰ 8pm-late), this futuristic penthouse has a surreal moon roof that retracts as you find your groove in the laser-lit fog on the dance floor below. Glass tiles change color with the mood and beat of the music, whether DJs are

---

UNDER-THE-RADAR NIGHTSPOTS

> Foundation Room (opposite)
> Forty Deuce (p153)
> Poetry (below)
> Downtown Cocktail Room (p134)
> Fireside Lounge (p134)

---

spinning hip hop, rock or pop and retro mash-ups. Dress to impress.

⭐ PIRANHA

☎ 791-0100; www.gipsylv.net; 4633 Paradise Rd; cover free-$25; ⏰ 9pm-late; 🚌 108

The gay universe of the Fruit Loop orbits Sin City's sexiest gay nightclub, decked out with fireplace patios, aquariums and waterfalls, plus the luxurious 8½ Ultra Lounge. Expect outrageous theme parties. There's often no cover before 11pm.

⭐ POETRY

☎ 369-4998; www.poetrynightclub .com; Forum Shops at Caesars Palace, 3500 Las Vegas Blvd S; cover $20-40; ⏰ 10pm-4am Thu-Sun; Ⓜ Flamingo/ Caesars Palace

Real urban beats at this mansion-esque hideaway may peak earlier than at other clubs, but there's rarely a long line. Hip hop and R&B DJs take you straight through the weekend, with celebs like rap star E-40 in the crowd. Strict dress code.

LAS VEGAS

PLAY

POLLY ESTHER'S
☎ 889-1980; www.pollyesthers.com;
Stratosphere, 2000 Las Vegas Blvd S;
cover $20, incl unlimited drinks $40;
🕑 10pm-4am Wed-Sat; Ⓜ Sahara
A chain megaclub, retro-minded
Polly Esther's takes nostalgic trips
back to the 1970's *Saturday Night
Fever*, the '80s Culture Club, Nerve
Ana for the '90s and the Suite
2000 ultra lounge. Short lines, no
hassles, and a ghetto-fabulous
crowd that couldn't care less what
you're wearing.

PURE
☎ 731-7873; www.purethenightclub
.com; Caesars Palace, 3570 Las Vegas
Blvd S; cover $20-40; 🕑 10pm-4am Tue
& Fri-Sun; Ⓜ Flamingo/Caesars Palace
With gorgeous female DJs, this
chic modern club electrifies with
its hues of electric blue, white
and silver. Crowds of fine young
thangs lounge inside a labyrinth
of rooms that feel a lot like LA,
and which lead to a gorgeous
Strip-view patio. Strict dress code.

STONEY'S ROCKIN' COUNTRY
☎ 435-2855; www.stoneysrockin
country.com; 9151 Las Vegas Blvd S;
cover $10; 🕑 7pm-late Thu-Sun; 🚌 117
Yeehaw! It's Vegas' biggest
country-and-western dance hall
and saloon, where a lustful crowd
stares slack-jawed at the bikini bull
riding. With DJs or live music every
weekend and a wide-open dance
floor, it's a rowdy place to kick up
your cowboy boots.

TAO
☎ 388-8588; www.taolasvegas
.com; Grand Canal Shoppes, Venetian,
3355 Las Vegas Blvd S; cover $10-40;
🕑 10pm-late Thu & Fri, 9:30pm-late Sat;
Ⓜ Harrah's/Imperial Palace
Modeled after the Asian-themed
NYC club, here svelte, nearly
naked go-go girls covered only
by strategically placed flowers
splash in bathtubs while another
in yogi garb assumes the lotus
position on a pedestal high above
the risqué dance floor, where Paris
Hilton lookalikes forego enlight-
enment to bump-and-grind to
earthy hip hop instead.

⭐ PRODUCTION SHOWS
The most in-demand tix are for
Cirque du Soleil extravaganzas
and straight-off-Broadway musicals. Old-school shows involve
minimal plot with a variety of
kitschy song, dance and magic
numbers. A grab-bag of erotically
themed shows, from rock musicals
to late-night vampire revues, are
rarely worth the money.

⚡ BETTE MIDLER
☎ 731-7110, 877-723-8836; www
.caesarspalace.com; Caesars Palace,
3570 Las Vegas Blvd S; tickets $95-250;
🕐 7:30pm Tue-Wed & Fri-Sun;
Ⓜ Flamingo/Caesars Palace
Backed by her 'Kiss My Brass' band,
the Divine Miss M brings her award-
winning voice and plenty of sass
to the stage once ruled by Céline
Dion. Cher is booked to play the
Palace soon. When the divas are
indisposed, Elton John sells out the
stage with his biographical retro-
'70s pop fantasia *The Red Piano*.

⚡ CRAZY HORSE PARIS
☎ 891-7777, 877-880-0880; www
.mgmgrand.com; MGM Grand, 3799 Las
Vegas Blvd S; tickets from $49; 🕐 8pm &
10:30pm Wed-Mon; Ⓜ MGM Grand
Za-za-zoom. At the artiest topless
show in town, the 100% red room's
intimate bordello feel oozes sex
appeal. Onstage, balletic dancers
straight from Paris' Crazy Horse
Saloon perform cabaret numbers
interspersed with voyeuristic and
humorous *l'art du nu* vignettes and
black-and-white film clips.

⚡ CRISS ANGEL: BELIEVE
☎ 262-4400, 800-557-7428; www
.cirquedusoleil.com; Luxor, 3900 Las
Vegas Blvd S; tickets $59-150;
🕐 7pm & 10pm Fri-Tue; 🚌 Deuce
The peripatetic French-Canadian
circus troupe Cirque du Soleil

mixes high-adrenaline stunts, surreal postmodern fantasy and dark,
dreamy magical illusions with
pop-star illusionist Criss Angel,
who stars as a Victorian lord beset
by buxom beauties.

⚡ FOLIES BERGÈRE
☎ 739-2222, 800-829-9034; www
.tropicanalv.com; Tropicana, 3801 Las
Vegas Blvd S; tickets $65-76; 🕐 7:30pm
(covered) & 10pm (topless) Mon, Wed &
Thu, 8:30pm (topless) Tue & Fri, 7:30 &
10pm (topless) Sat; Ⓜ MGM Grand
A gaudy tribute to the Parisian
Music Hall, Vegas' longest-
running production still has some
of the most beautiful showgirls
in town. Sticking to a formulaic
Francophile theme, over-the-top
song-and-dance numbers include
the inevitable can-can routine,
plus a comedic juggler to lighten
it up.

⚡ JUBILEE!
☎ 967-4567, 800-237-7469; www
.ballyslasvegas.com; Bally's, 3645 Las
Vegas Blvd S; tickets $48-110; 🕐 7:30pm
& 10:30pm Sat-Thu; Ⓜ Bally's/Paris
Girls, girls, girls! It's a showgirl
production that Vegas wouldn't
be Vegas without. As it started, so
does it end: with lots of knockers,
twinkling rhinestones and enormous headdresses on display. If
you can forgive the giant helping
of cheese, it's a riot.

PEEK BEHIND THE SHOWGIRLS' CURTAIN

Bally's **Backstage Tour** (☎ 946-4567, 800-237-7469) runs one-hour backstage tours of its long-running spectacular, Donn Arden's *Jubilee!* (p145). The tours ($15, with show-ticket purchase $10) offer a behind-the-scenes look at the hidden lives of Las Vegas showgirls and chorus boys, starting at 11am Monday, Wednesday and Saturday.

⭐ KÀ

☎ 891-7777, 877-880-0880; http://ka.com; MGM Grand, 3799 Las Vegas Blvd S; tickets adult $69-150, child $35-75; ⌚ 7pm & 9:30pm Tue-Sat; Ⓜ MGM Grand; ♿

Cirque du Soleil makes this sensuous but impossible-to-follow story of imperial twins, mysterious destinies, love and conflict a hot ticket. Instead of a stage, there's a grid of moving platforms for a frenzy of martial arts–inspired performances. Premium seats hold court at the back.

⭐ LA CAGE

☎ 794-9433, 877-892-7469; www.rivierahotel.com; Riviera, 2901 Las Vegas Blvd S; tickets $75; ⌚ 7:30pm Wed-Mon; 🚍 Deuce

In this mainstream female-impersonator revue, the award-winning Frank Marino (who had a cameo in *Miss Congeniality 2*) acts as a catty Joan Rivers, dispensing naughty jokes and remarks between mostly lip-synched impersonations of Diana Ross, Cher and Liza Minnelli.

⭐ LA RÊVE

☎ 770-9966, 888-320-7110; www.wynnlasvegas.com; Wynn Las Vegas, 3131 Las Vegas Blvd S; tickets $99-179; ⌚ 7pm & 9:30pm Fri-Mon; 🚍 Deuce

Aquatic acrobatic feats by scuba-certified performers are the centerpiece of this theater, which holds a one-million-gallon swimming pool; critics call it a less-inspiring version of Cirque's O. Beware: the cheap seats are in the 'splash zone'. The VIP 'Indulgence' package offers champagne and chocolate-covered strawberries, as well as personal video monitors for close ups of the performance and behind-the-scenes glimpses.

⭐ LEGENDS IN CONCERT

☎ 794-3261, 800-351-7400; www.imperialpalace.com; Imperial Palace, 3535 Las Vegas Blvd S; tickets incl 1 drink $50-60; ⌚ 7:30pm & 10pm Mon-Sat; Ⓜ Harrah's/Imperial Palace; ♿

Vegas' top pop-star impersonator show features real talent – there is no lip-synching allowed. Video screens beside the stage show real-life concert clips of the

PLAY

performers, while the back-up dancers boogie up a *Saturday Night Fever* storm.

⭐ LOVE
☎ 792-7777, 800-963-9634; www .cirquedusoleil.com; Mirage, 3400 Las Vegas Blvd S; tickets $94-150; ☾ 7pm & 10pm Thu-Mon; Ⓜ Harrah's/Imperial Palace; ♿
Another smash hit from Cirque du Soleil, LOVE started off as the brainchild of the late George Harrison. Using Abbey Road master tapes, the show psychedelically fuses the musical legacy of the Beatles with Cirque's high-energy dancers and, of course, the troupe's signature aerial acrobats. With 360-degree seating, everyone gets a good view.

⭐ MYSTÈRE
☎ 894-7722, 800-392-1999; www .cirquedusoleil.com; TI (Treasure Island), 3300 Las Vegas Blvd S; tickets $60-95; ☾ 7pm & 9:30pm Sat-Wed; 🚌 Deuce; ♿
What Dali did for painting, Cirque du Soleil aims to do for the stage. An oddball celebration of life begins with a pair of babies making their way in a world filled with weird creatures. A misguided clown's humorous antics are interspersed with agile feats of acrobats, aerialists and

dancers. It's the cheapest Cirque ticket in town.

⭐ PHANTOM
☎ 414-9000, 866-641-7469; www .venetian.com; Venetian, 3355 Las Vegas Blvd S; tickets $69-158; ☾ 7pm Mon-Sat, 9:30pm Mon & Sat; Ⓜ Harrah's/Imperial Palace; ♿
A drop-dead gorgeous theater mimics the opulent 19th-century Parisian opera house where this haunting musical about a doomed love triangle takes place. Boastfully renamed 'The Las Vegas Spectacular,' the Strip's version stars all-new special effects, from an onstage lake to exploding fireworks above. The VIP experience buys a backstage tour.

⭐ THE RAT PACK IS BACK!
☎ 386-2444; www.ratpackvegas .com; Plaza, 1 Main St; tickets $57-88; ☾ 7:30pm Mon-Fri, 7:30pm & 10pm Sat; 🚌 Deuce
Capitalizing on Rat Pack nostalgia, the show faithfully replicates the gang's routines, right down to the same songs, politically incorrect jokes and embarrassing behavior by Marilyn Monroe. Ol' Blue Eyes looks convincing, but you'll fall in love with Dino and the fantastic live band. If only the crowd had more young hipsters and fewer cranky senior citizens, it'd be aces.

⭐ SPAS & SALONS

Some day spas are reserved exclusively for hotel guests, especially on weekends. Day-use fees ($20 to $45) are normally waived for those receiving treatments ($100 to $200 per hour). Many spas have fitness facilities (bring workout clothes and shoes) and full-service beauty salons.

BATHHOUSE

☎ 877-632-9636; www.thehotelat mandalaybay.com; THEhotel at Mandalay Bay, 3950 Las Vegas Blvd S; ⏰ 6am-8:30pm; 🚌 Deuce

Seducing both sexes, this $25-million minimalist Asian-inspired spa offers redwood saunas, eucalyptus steam rooms and Ayurvedic herbal baths. Organic skincare products include an 'aromapothecary' of massage oils blended to match your personality.

CANYON RANCH SPACLUB

☎ 414-3600, 877-220-2688; www .canyonranch.com; 4th fl, Grand Canal Shoppes, Venetian, 3355 Las Vegas Blvd S; ⏰ 5:30am-10pm, café 7am-6pm; 🚌 Harrah's/Imperial Palace

Popular for side-by-side couples' treatments, this health-minded place offers over 100 activities – from Ayurvedic massage to rock climbing – all priced à la carte. Rates are cheaper midweek. The Palazzo (p54) branch features 'Aquavana' thermal spa baths, experiential rains, a wave room, salt grotto and snow cave.

Bathhouse offers the ultimate in pampering. Go on...

LAS VEGAS

PLAY

DRIFT SPA & HAMMAM
☎ 944-3219; www.palmsplace.com;
Palms Place, Palms, 4381 W Flamingo Rd;
🕐 6am-9pm; 🚌 202
Make that nasty hangover disappear and let your mind unwind at this glam spa. Bathe yourself in steam at the co-ed traditional Turkish hammam (sorry, *not* clothing-optional), dip into the hot-soaking and cold-plunge pools, and get lost in the garden, where couples' treatment rooms are lit by aromatherapy candles after dark. Thermal detox and Ayurvedic health remedies are available on demand.

KIM VŌ SALON
☎ 791-7474; www.kimvo.com; Mirage, 3400 Las Vegas Blvd S; 🕐 9am-7pm;
Ⓜ Harrah's/Imperial Palace
Feel absolutely fabulous at celebrity stylist Kim Vō's salon while you get a champagne hair rinse under a disco ball or a makeover from the magic man himself, who has worked on pro athletes and US presidents.

QUA BATHS & SPA
☎ 731-7776, 866-782-0655; www .harrahs.com/qua; 2nd fl, Augustus Tower, Caesars Palace, 3570 Las Vegas Blvd S; 🕐 6am-8pm; Ⓜ Flamingo/ Caesars Palace
Social spa-going is encouraged at Qua, which evokes the ancient Roman rituals of indulgent bathing. The spa's gossipy public areas include a tea lounge, herbal steam room, cedar sauna and arctic ice room, where artificial snowflakes fall. On the men's side, there's a barber spa and big-screen live-sports TVs.

RED ROCK SPA
☎ 797-7878, 866-363-2872; www .redrocklasvegas.com; Red Rock Casino Resort Spa, 11011 W Charleston Blvd at I-215; 🕐 8am-8pm; 🚌 206
Far-flung west of the Strip, this chic spa emphasizes holistic healing practices and is best known for its adventure-spa menu, which features guided rock climbing in nearby Red Rock Canyon (p160). Order a specialty Thai massage or get rubbed down 'on the rocks' with heated river stones.

⭐ SPORTS
Although Vegas doesn't have any professional sports franchises, it's a city of die-hard sports fans. You can wager on just about anything at casinos' race and sports books (p39). Nearly every watering hole runs Monday Night Football specials, including downtown's Triple 7 brewpub (p137).
World-class championship boxing draws in fans from all over the globe; take a look at

www.boxinginlasvegas.com for the latest news, ringside pics and fight schedules.

Auto racing at the Las Vegas Motor Speedway is enormously popular, especially during Nascar Weekend in March. The premier rodeo event of the year is the Wrangler National Finals Rodeo (p132), held every December. **UNLV Runnin' Rebels** (☎ 739-3267, 866-388-3267; www.unlvtickets.com) college football and basketball teams enjoy a patriotic local following. With a googly-eyed alien mascot, the minor-league **Las Vegas**

51s (☎ 386-7200; www.lv51.com; Cashman Field, 850 Las Vegas Blvd N) baseball team, a franchise of the MLB Los Angeles Dodgers, plays home games from April to August. Feeding the NHL Calgary Flames, the minor-league **Las Vegas Wranglers** (☎ 471-7825; www.lasvegaswranglers.com) ice-hockey team faces off at the Orleans Arena from October to May. If you adore watching bitchy, buxom girls on wheels, there's the riotous **Sin City Rollergirls** (www.lasvegasderbygirls.com; Las Vegas Roller Hockey Center, 953 E Sahara Ave) roller derby team.

FORE!

There are dozens of spectacular golf courses in the Vegas Valley, most within 10 miles of the Strip. Golf season is in full swing from fall through spring (summers are just too darn hot!). For green-fee discounts and last-minute tee-time availability, contact **Las Vegas Preferred Tee Times** (☎ 877-255-7277; www.lvptt.com).

Angel Park (☎ 254-4653, 888-446-5358; www.angelpark.com; 100 S Rampart Blvd) Arnold Palmer–designed championship 18-hole courses, plus the 12-hole, par-3 Cloud Nine course (which is partially lit for night play).

Badlands (☎ 363-0754; www.badlandsgc.com; 9119 Alta Dr) Three 9-hole Troon Golf courses present the ultimate bad-ass desert challenge, with ball-chewing turf and unforgiving layouts.

Las Vegas Paiute Golf Resort (☎ 658-1400, 800-711-2833; www.lvpaiutegolf.com; 10325 Nu-Way Kaiv Blvd, off US95) A trio of scenic Pete Dye–designed courses in the Spring Mountains outside town.

Royal Links (☎ 450-8123, 888-427-6678; www.royallinksgolfclub.com; 5995 E Vegas Valley) A castle-like clubhouse (with a pub!) leads onto an 18-hole course inspired by famous British Open greens. Tiger Woods scored a record-setting 67 here.

Tournament Players Clubs Las Vegas (TPC; ☎ 256-2500; www.tpc.com/lasvegas; 9851 Canyon Run Dr) A PGA Tour stop, the Canyons course incorporates native desert vegetation, which requires minimal irrigation. It's also a certified Audubon cooperative sanctuary.

SPORTS & CONCERT MEGA VENUES

Las Vegas Motor Speedway (☎ 644-4444, 800-644-4444; www.lvms.com; 7000 Las Vegas Blvd N) Nascar, Indy racing, drag racing and race car ride-alongs (p83).

Mandalay Bay Events Center (☎ 632-7580; www.mandalaybay.com; 3950 Las Vegas Blvd S; 🚌 Deuce) Boxing, ultimate fighting and headliner concerts.

MGM Grand Garden Arena (☎ 891-8777, 877-880-0880; www.mgmgrand.com; 3799 Las Vegas Blvd S; Ⓜ MGM Grand) Boxing, superstar concerts and tennis.

Orleans Arena (☎ 284-7777, 888-234-2334; www.orleansarena.com; Orleans, 4500 W Tropicana Ave; 🚌 201) Boxing, hockey, motorsports and concerts.

Sam Boyd Stadium (☎ 739-3267, 866-388-3267; www.unlvtickets.com; 7000 E Russell Rd) UNLV college football, motorsports and concerts.

South Point Events Center (☎ 797-8005; www.southpointeventscenter.com; 9777 Las Vegas Blvd S; 🚌 117) Equestrian events, boxing, motorcycle races and monster-truck jams.

Thomas & Mack Center (☎ 739-3267, 866-388-3267; www.unlvtickets.com; UNLV campus, S Swenson St & Tropicana Ave; 🚌 108, 201) College basketball, boxing, concerts and rodeos.

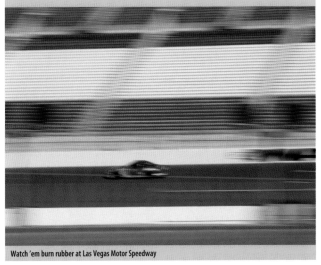

Watch 'em burn rubber at Las Vegas Motor Speedway

GIRLS JUST WANNA HAVE FUN

The dancers at Rio's **Chippendales Theater** (☎ 777-7776; www.riolas vegas.com; admission $40-50) seem more concerned with basking in the spotlight than giving the girls a good time. Private sky boxes, Flirt cocktail lounge and a plush bathroom with a 'gossip pit' are the icing on the hunky cake. You can touch the lovely lads of Excalibur's **Thunder Down Under** (☎ 597-7600; www.excalibur.com; admission $40-50), who provide non-stop fun and flirting. At Polly Esther's nightclub (p144), VH1's award-winning male revue **American Storm** (☎ 383-5210; www.stratospherehotel.com; tickets $50) takes it off almost nightly.

 STRIP CLUBS

Vegas is the original adult Disney-land. Prostitution may be illegal, but there are plenty of places offering the illusion of sex on de-mand. Unescorted women are not welcome at most clubs, especially not on busy nights. Bring cash for tips.

⭐ OLYMPIC GARDEN

☎ 385-9361; www.ogvegas.com; 1531 Las Vegas Blvd S; cover $30; ⏲ 24hr; 🚌 Deuce

The unpretentious OG wins high marks from topless-club aficionados – and the nickname 'Silicone Valley' from the competi-tion. Up to 50 dancers work the rooms at any given time, so there's something to please everyone. Studs strip upstairs for the ladies Wednesday through Sunday nights.

⭐ SAPPHIRE

☎ 796-6000; www.sapphirelasvegas .com; 3025 S Industrial Rd; cover $30-50; ⏲ 24hr; 🚌 119

Everything is larger-than-life at the 'world's largest adult entertainment complex,' with a stable of thousands of entertain-ers and VIP skyboxes overlooking the showroom that's cheesily dominated by a story-high martini glass. Beefy men strip upstairs in the Playgirl Club on Friday and Saturday nights.

⭐ SCORES LAS VEGAS

☎ 367-4000; www.lvscores.com; 3355 S Procyon St; cover $30; ⏲ 24hr

The NYC strip-club chain that Howard Stern raves about has taken over a building that looks like a miniature replica of Caesars Palace. Celebrity actors and pro athletes often drop by, though you probably won't catch a glimpse of 'em – they get their own private entrance. The pre-mium cigar menu is superb. Look for flirty couples' packages.

SEAMLESS
☎ 227-5200; www.seamlessclub.com; 4740 S Arville St; cover $20-30; ⏰ 24hr; 🚌 104, 201

Erasing the thin line between Sin City's strip clubs and night-clubs, this high-concept spot switches gears 'seamlessly' at 4am every night, when gorgeous exotic dancers don teensy-weensy cock-tail waitress outfits for a DJ-driven after-hours dance party for both sexes that keeps going strong till after dawn.

ULTRA LOUNGES & AFTER HOURS
The strip club Seamless (listed above) transforms itself nightly into a sensual after-hours party spot.

DRAI'S
☎ 737-0555; www.drais.net; Bill's Gamblin' Hall & Saloon, 3595 Las Vegas Blvd S; cover $20-30; ⏰ midnight-dawn Thu-Sun; 🚌 Flamingo/Caesars Palace

Ready for a scene straight outta Hollywood? Things don't really get going until after 4am here, when DJs spinning progressive discs keep the fashion plates who drape themselves on overstuffed sofas from being too discontented. Strict dress code.

FORTY DEUCE
☎ 632-9442; www.fortydeuce.com; lower level, Mandalay Place, 3930 Las Vegas Blvd S; cover $25; ⏰ 10:30pm-dawn Thu-Sun; 🚌 Deuce

A speakeasy vibe pervades this opulent but petite bi-level club. Ignore the bachelorette antics and feast your eyes on the smoking-hot burlesque acts that are backed up by a brassy three-piece jazz combo or rock 'n' roll band. Acts appear on stage several times nightly, starting before midnight.

GHOSTBAR
☎ 942-6832; http://ghostbar-las-vegas.n9negroup.com; 55th fl, Palms Tower, Palms, 4321 W Flamingo Rd; cover $20; ⏰ 8pm-late; 🚌 202

With its 360-degree panoramas and sci-fi decor, the Palms' 55th-floor watering hole pulls in a clubby crowd thick with hip-hop stars and pro athletes. The line-up of hoochie mamas and wannabe gangstas can be tiresome, but the views are to die for. Dress to kill.

PUSSYCAT DOLLS LOUNGE
☎ 731-7873; www.pcdlounge.com; Caesars Palace, 3570 Las Vegas Blvd S; cover $10-30; ⏰ 10:30pm-4am Tue-Sat; 🅜 Flamingo/Caesars Palace

Lingerie-clad ladies do a little aer-ial swinging, play rub-a-dub-dub in a tub and flaunt sexy song-and-dance numbers just about every half hour. Look for Hollywood

ALL WET

Las Vegas' outrageous pool-party season heats up the summer. Think of it as Ibiza in the desert: outdoor clubs with bikini-clad models, bumpin' DJs and bottle service. Expect hefty cover charges and long lines; queue early, especially on weekends. Our fave places to chill out poolside:

Bare (Mirage; p52) Adults-only pool lounge with mod chaise lounges, palm trees waving overhead, and cold fruit smoothies and hot tapas bites.

Ditch Fridays (Palms; p55) Skipping school or work has never seemed so seductive. An MTV-style, anything-goes atmosphere rules.

Rehab (Hard Rock; p48) A-list celebs, rock stars and costumed partiers are among the hoards lounging poolside on summer Sundays.

Tao Beach (Tao; p144) Tan yourself lying on daybeds or cool off inside high-tech cabañas that are outfitted with iPods and Xboxes.

Venus Pool Club (Caesars Palace; p43) Topless sunbathing, frozen grapes and towels, Evian misters and spa attendants define decadence.

celebs like Eva Longoria of *Desperate Housewives* making surprise appearances at this SoCal import. Fashionable attire required.

REVOLUTION LOUNGE
☎ 692-8383; www.thebeatlesrevolutionlounge.com; Mirage, 3400 Las Vegas Blvd S; cover $5-$20; ☾ 10pm-4am; Ⓜ Harrah's/Imperial Palace
Fans of the original Fab Four can drop into this psychedelic Beatles-themed ultra lounge created by Cirque du Soleil. DJs spin just about everything, from down-tempo house, Brit pop, hip hop and world music fusion to mash-ups of classic rock and '80s new wave. The no-cover Abbey Road Bar out front opens at noon daily.

V BAR
☎ 414-3200; www.venetian.com; Venetian, 3355 Las Vegas Blvd S; ☾ 5pm-2am Sun-Wed, 5pm-3am Thu-Sat; Ⓜ Harrah's/Imperial Palace
Fashionistas air-kiss inside this glam lounge, where low-key house tunes, seductively low lighting, secluded sofas and sturdy martinis encourage intimate behavior among strangers.

WASTED SPACE
☎ 693-4040; www.hartswastedspace.com; Hard Rock, 4455 Paradise Rd; cover $10-25; ☾ 8pm-4am Tue-Sun; 🚌 108, 202
Celebs packed the opening of Wasted Space, a rock 'n' roll lounge marked with tattoo-style designs, from motocross legend and night-club promoter Corey Hart. It's a chill place to hang with friends till dawn.

>OUT OF TOWN

Explore the breathtaking Red Rock Canyon (p160), only a half-hour drive from the Strip

OUT OF TOWN

GRAND CANYON NATIONAL PARK

The Grand Canyon is the USA's best-known natural attraction. Measuring over 275 miles long and more than a mile deep, it's an incredible spectacle of Technicolor rock strata. After initially being dismissed by Spanish conquistadors and Western pioneers as little more than an obstacle to exploration, in the late 19th century the canyon drew miners bent on exploiting its natural resources. Later tourists arrived seeking a romanticized wilderness ideal as they embraced the canyon's beauty. When President Theodore Roosevelt visited in 1903, he sagely remarked, 'You cannot improve on it.'

Carved by the Colorado River, the canyon's peaks, buttes and rims give access to fantastic vistas. Descending into its depths on hiking and mule-riding trails reveals an amazing variety of landscape, wildlife and climates. If your time is limited, flightseeing day trips from Las Vegas (often combined with flyovers of Hoover Dam and Lake Mead, and a bus tour of the South Rim) can introduce you to this gobstopping hole in the ground.

Although the canyon's rims are only 10 miles apart as the condor flies, it's a 215-mile, five-hour drive on narrow roads between the South and North

The stunning vista of the Grand Canyon from the South Rim at Hopi Point

Rim visitor centers. The **South Rim** is the most popular jumping-off point for exploring the national park, where there is no escaping the crowds between May and September. Though the South Rim receives over 90% of the four-million people who visit the park each year, the **North Rim** is actually a bit closer to Vegas, and it's a lot closer to Zion and Bryce Canyon National Parks.

Approaching the South Rim, **Mather Point** near Canyon View Information Plaza gives you an exhilarating first look at the canyon's grandeur. After stretching your legs, drive north to **Grand Canyon Village**. Peruse Native American crafts inside **Hopi House**, designed by innovative Western architect Mary Colter; have cocktails on the back porch of the majestic **El Tovar Hotel**; and peruse the art displays inside **Kolb Studio**. For panoramic views of the canyon's geological layer cake, head over to **Yavapai Information Station**.

Of course, the foremost attraction is the canyon rim itself, paralleled on the south side by a 33-mile scenic road. The canyon dips in and out of view as the road passes through the piñon-juniper and ponderosa pine forests. Pullouts along the way offer jaw-dropping views, and interpretive signs explain about natural history. Between March and November, only shuttle buses may travel along Hermit Rd west of the village. To the east, Desert View Rd is open to cars year-round. The latter takes you past the 800-year-old pueblo ruins behind the **Tusayan Museum** of Native American history and culture, and the enchanting five-story-high **Desert View Watchtower**, which is the highest point on the South Rim. On the North Rim, rugged 4WD roads lead to more remote viewpoints.

To get away from the traffic, you can day-hike partway down to the Colorado River, or stay overnight at Phantom Ranch, where reservations are a must. Mule rides and river-rafting trips also require advance planning.

INFORMATION
Location 275 miles southeast of Las Vegas
Getting there 🚗 From the Strip: for South Rim (five hours), take I-15 south to I-215 east to US 93 south to I-40 east to AZ 64 north to Grand Canyon Village; North Rim is 265 miles (about 4½ hours) from Las Vegas via I-15 north to UT 9 east through Zion National Park to Alt-US 89 south to AZ 67 south
Contact ☎ 928-638-7888; www.nps.gov/grca
Cost per vehicle for a seven-day pass $25
When to go South Rim 🕐 24/7/365; North Rim 🕐 mid-May–mid-Oct
Eating South Rim: Arizona Room (☎ 928-638-2631; Bright Angel Lodge); North Rim: Grand Canyon Lodge Dining Room (☎ 928-638-2611)

HOOVER DAM, LAKE MEAD & VALLEY OF FIRE

Once the tallest in the world, the art-deco Hoover Dam is an engineering marvel, its graceful concrete curve filling a dramatic canyon backed by brilliant blue waters. The dam was built primarily to control floods on the lower Colorado River, which irrigates a million acres of land in the USA and half a million in Mexico.

Bus tours from Las Vegas are a good deal and guarantee a ticket for the tour, which lets you ride an elevator 50 stories down to see the massive power generators, then zoom back up to view the exhibit halls, outdoor spillways and Winged Figures of the Republic memorial.

When you tire of admiring the view and pretending to jump the railing (no terrorist jokes, please – that sort of thing is taken *very* seriously around here), backtrack a few miles to **Lake Mead National Recreation Area** (☎ 702-293-8906; www.nps.gov/lame; admission per car $5; 🕙 24hr), where a scenic shoreline drive passes hiking trails, beaches, marinas and birding spots, all the way up to Overton's **Lost City Museum** (☎ 702-397-2193; 721 S Moapa Valley Blvd; adult/child $3/free; 🕙 8:30am-4:30pm) of Native American culture. The museum is north of the turn-off to **Valley of Fire State Park** (☎ 702-397-2088; http://parks.nv.gov/vf.htm; admission per car $6; 🕙 24hr), a masterpiece of Southwest desert scenery with psychedelic sandstone carved by wind and water (**Atlatl Rock** has Native American petroglyphs, too). Detour to **White Domes**, passing **Rainbow Vista** and the side road to **Fire Canyon** and **Silica Dome** (where Captain Kirk perished in *Star Trek: Generations*).

INFORMATION
Location 30 miles southeast of Las Vegas
Getting there 🚗 From the Strip (45 minutes): I-15 south to I-215 east to I-515/US 93 & 95; follow US 93 east of Boulder City
Contact ☎ 702-494-2517; www.usbr.gov/lc/hooverdam
Cost Hoover Dam tours $8-11, parking garage $7
When to go Hoover Dam visitor center 🕙 9am-5pm (to 6pm in summer), last tickets sold 1hr before closing
Eating Milo's (☎ 702-293-9540; 538 Nevada Way, Boulder City)

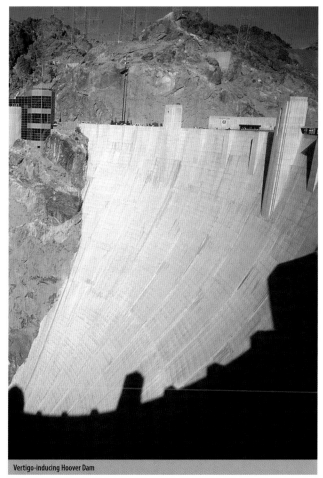
Vertigo-inducing Hoover Dam

RED ROCK CANYON

The 300-square-mile Red Rock Canyon National Conservation Area (pictured right) should be on everyone's must-see list, but fortunately isn't. The startling contrast between the Strip's artificial neon glow and the awesome nat-ural forces of the canyon can't be exaggerated.

Created about 65-million years ago, the canyon is more like a valley, with a steep, rugged escarpment rising 3000ft on its western edge. A 13-mile, one-way **scenic driving and cycling loop** passes by its most striking natural features and panoramic viewpoints. Rugged hiking trails lead to seasonal waterfalls. The **Calico Hills** area is the premier place for rock climb-ing. The popular **Willow Springs** picnic area offers nature walks. To ride 'em cowboy, make reservations with **Cowboy Trail Rides** (☎ 702-387-2457; www.cowboytrailrides.com).

Before reaching Red Rock Canyon, you'll drive by the dusty town of Blue Diamond, where **McGhie's Bike Outpost** (☎ 702-875-4820; www.bikeoutpost .com; 16 Cottonwood #B; call for hours) is a one-stop shop for rentals (per day $35), guided tours around Red Rock Canyon, and directions to more than 125 miles of single track in the Cottonwood Valley and Black Velvet areas. North along NV 159, **Spring Mountain Ranch State Park** (☎ 702-875-4141; http://parks.nv.gov/smr.htm; admission per car $5; 8am-dusk, visitor center 10am-4pm), once owned by eccentric billionaire Howard Hughes, offers nature walks, ranch tours and historical exhibits. Nearby **Bonnie Springs** (☎ 702-875-4191; www.bonniesprings.com; 1 Gunfighter Lane; admission per car $20; 10:30am-5pm, to 6pm in summer), the scene of countless B-movie shoots, is a touristy sideshow for the kiddies.

INFORMATION

Location 20 miles west of Las Vegas
Getting there 🚗 From the Strip (30 minutes): I-15 south to Blue Diamond Rd (NV 160), then west to NV 159
Contact ☎ 702-515-5350; www.redrockcanyonlv.org
Cost per car/bicycle $5/free
When to go Visitor center 8am-4:30pm, scenic loop 6am-5pm Nov-Feb, 6am-7pm Mar & Oct, 6am-8pm Apr-Sep
Eating Hash House A Go Go (p126), Salt Lick BBQ (p128)

TAKE A TOUR

Free Strip hotel pick-ups and drop-offs are included with most tours; check online for deep discounts. Hour-long air tours of the Grand Canyon cost from $115 per person; day-long air/ground combos run from $230 to $315, and premier helicopter tours landing on the canyon's floor fetch over $350. For city tours, see p193.

Adventure Las Vegas (☎ 888-867-6259; www.adventurelasvegas.com; tours $89-539; ☼ reservations 24hr) One-stop shop for adventure tours; arranges everything from sunset horseback rides to kayaking Lake Mead.

Black Canyon River Adventures (☎ 294-1414, 800-455-3490; www.blackcanyon adventures.com; Hacienda Hotel & Casino, US 93, Boulder City; tours $51-119) Take a three-hour motor-assisted raft journey down the Colorado River, launching from the base of Hoover Dam.

Boulder City Outfitters (☎ 293-1190, 800-748-3702; www.bouldercityoutfitters.com; 1631 Industrial Rd, Boulder City; guided mountain-biking & hiking tours $100, guided kayak tours $163, canoe & kayak rental per day $35-55, mountain-bike rental per half-/full-day from $25/40) Guided kayak tours (two-person minimum) launch from the base of Hoover Dam, with stops at hot springs and waterfalls; shuttle service available for DIY paddlers.

Escape Adventures (☎ 596-2953, 800-596-2953; www.escapeadventures.com; weekend trips from $399) Escape the city's neon jungle for a mountain-biking, road-cycling, hiking or multi-sport adventure tour of Red Rock Canyon or nearby national parks.

Gray Line (☎ 384-1234, 800-634-6579; www.graylinelasvegas.com; tours $48-182) Reputable tour-bus operator offers a variety of excursions to Hoover Dam, Red Rock Canyon and the Grand Canyon, as well as Colorado River floats.

Papillon Grand Canyon Helicopters (☎ 736-7243, 888-635-7272; www.papillon.com; McCarran Executive Terminal, 275 E Tropicana Ave; bus/flightseeing tours from $86/259) Vegas' original helicopter-flightseeing outfitter does luxury tours of the Grand Canyon; its motorcoach tours of the South Rim stop en route at Hoover Dam.

Pink Jeep Tours (☎ 895-6777, 888-900-4480; www.pinkjeeplasvegas.com; half-day tours $79-124, full-day tours $209-565) Arranges small-group trips to Hoover Dam, Red Rock Canyon, Valley of Fire, Mt Charleston, Death Valley and Zion National Park. The Grand Canyon combo tour features short helicopter and pontoon-boat rides.

Las Vegas is the gambling capital of the world. That said, it's a sure bet you'll find much more to amuse yourself in Sin City than playing cards or pulling slots. To strip off the wildly different masks that this postmodern desert oasis wears, flip through our handy miniguides.

Take a breather from the one-armed bandits and check out downtown street artists

ACCOMMODATIONS

Vegas hits the jackpot, with over 135,000 guest rooms. Even if a bankroll isn't burning a hole in your pocket, a little luxury can be had more cheaply here than almost anywhere else in the world. Of course an exquisite penthouse villa overlooking Las Vegas Blvd (aka the Strip), with perks such as 24-hour butler service, costs thousands of dollars per night.

On your first trip to Las Vegas, almost any casino hotel on the Strip will bedazzle, but don't go by name recognition alone. The Center Strip is where most of the magnificent megaresorts and the hottest action is, and you'll pay for it. The South Strip is a comfy compromise: you'll get the full Vegas experience, but for less dough. Some famous casino hotels on the North Strip have the most disappointing rooms and location. Downtown is for local gamblers and penny-pinchers who've tired of the Strip scene. Outlying-area hotels offer some deals, if you're willing to make the trip.

Whatever you do, don't arrive without a reservation. It's amazing how often every hotel in town is booked solid. Year-round, room rates average

Need a place to stay? Find and book it at lonelyplanet.com. More than 43 properties are featured for Las Vegas – each personally visited, thoroughly reviewed and happily recommended by a Lonely Planet author. From hostels to high-end hotels, we've hunted out the places that will bring you unique and special experiences. Read independent reviews by authors and other travelers, and get practical information including amenities, maps and photos. Then reserve your room simply and securely via our online booking service. It's all at www.lonelyplanet.com/hotels.

50% less from Sunday through Thursday nights. Unless you're on a junket, avoid visiting during the biggest conventions, when hotel rates shoot sky-high. The slowest times of year are during the excruciatingly hot summer (June, July and August) and between Thanksgiving and Christmas. If you're claustrophobic, pass on New Year's Eve and other major holidays (p192).

If you're looking for a lower rate or want to stay at a hotel that's sold out, check back in a few days or a week or two. Sometimes you can suddenly reserve rooms for much less than you'd been quoted before. It also pays to check with your booked hotel a week or so in advance to see if the rates you were quoted have changed, and if they've fallen, ask that your reservation rate be lowered, too.

WEB RESOURCES

Discounted room rates are most easily found on the hotels' own websites or at online travel discounters such as www.travelworm.com or www.trip res.com. The **Las Vegas Convention & Visitors Authority** (☎ 877-847-4858; www.visit lasvegas.com) can help with last-minute accommodations.

LAS VEGAS' HIPPEST HOTELS

> Hard Rock (www.hardrockhotel.com)
> THEhotel at Mandalay Bay
  (www.thehotelatmandalaybay.com)
> Palms Place (www.palmsplace.com)
> Red Rock (www.redrocklasvegas.com)
> Signature at MGM Grand
  (www.signaturemgmgrand.com)

LAS VEGAS' MOST LUXURIOUS SUITES

> Palazzo (www.palazzolasvegas.com)
> Palms Place (www.palmsplace.com)
> Skylofts at MGM Grand
  (www.skyloftsmgmgrand.com)
> Venetian (www.venetian.com)
> Wynn Las Vegas
  (www.wynnlasvegas.com)

LAS VEGAS' COOLEST HOTEL POOLS

> Bellagio (www.bellagio.com)
> Caesars Palace
  (www.caesarspalace.com)
> Flamingo (www.flamingolasvegas.com)
> Mandalay Bay
  (www.mandalaybay.com)
> MGM Grand (www.mgmgrand.com)

LAS VEGAS' BEST BARGAIN HOTELS

> Golden Nugget
  (www.goldennugget.com)
> Main Street Station
  (www.mainstreetcasino.com)
> Orleans (www.orleanscasino.com)
> Sahara (www.saharavegas.com)
> South Point
  (www.southpointcasino.com)

Top left No need to leave your hotel room at the Signature at MGM Grand

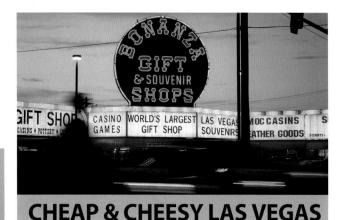

CHEAP & CHEESY LAS VEGAS

Elvis and Liberace have long gone to their graves, and Siegfried and Roy are no longer performing on the Strip with their white tigers, but Las Vegas still has plenty of wacky and way-out, tacky and trashy stuff to see and do. Best of all, much of it won't cost you a thing.

Some critics lament that everything in Las Vegas is in outrageously bad taste, and, of course, that's often true. But that's something to celebrate, too. It's as much fun to dive into the city's unbelievably campy depths as it is to aim for its high-rollin' luxury heights.

So, when you're down to your last dime, don't despair. Spend all day watching the gob-stopping free casino spectaculars (p80) and inhaling the (almost free) food and drinks. Did you know they'll serve you free booze even if you're just playing the 'Penny Alley' slot machines? It's true.

Speed down the Strip, which is a free-for-all freak show, day and night. Gawk at the Mirage's exploding faux-Polynesian volcano (p81). Get your free kicks watching the sexy hijinks of the Sirens of TI (p81) mock pirate battle. Check out Marilyn Monroe and Elvis impersonators performing at the Imperial Palace (p78).

Hold-outs from the 1950s and '60s, a few kitschy casino hotels survive at the far north end of the Strip. Circus Circus (p44) definitely wins the prize for the cheesiest casino theme. Pick up a 'fun book' full of discount coupons at the hilariously tacky Slots A' Fun (p80) next door. Across the street, grab a tropical drink at the garishly neon-lit Fireside Lounge (p134), which is attached to the Peppermill casino's 24-hour coffee shop. If you're still rarin' to go for a low-roller's ride, there's no better place to keep the party going strong than on downtown's Fremont Street Experience (p80).

Last but not least, pay your respects to the maestro of flamboyant kitsch, Liberace, at his off-Strip memorial museum (p79), where fanatical 'Red Hatters' keep the candles of his outrageous shrine burning bright.

VEGAS' KITSCHIEST SOUVENIRS
> At-home gaming paraphernalia from the Gamblers General Store (p99)
> Authentic Old Vegas memorabilia from Main Street Antiques (p98)
> Casino-themed cocktail glasses (eg plastic Eiffel Tower from Paris Las Vegas, colorful ceramic showgirl stein from Bally's)

> G-string, go-go boots or an erotic toy from a naughty novelty shop (p90)
> Showgirl's feather boa from Rainbow Feather Dyeing Co (p99)

CHEESIEST VEGAS ATTRACTIONS
> Bonanza Gifts (p98)
> Circus Circus Midway (p80)
> Fremont Street Experience (p80)
> Liberace Museum (p79)
> Slots A' Fun (p80)

Top left Looking for that snow globe to complete the collection? Visit Bonanza Gifts (p98) **Above** Dice for every occasion at Gamblers General Store (p99)

LAS VEGAS FOR LOVERS

There must be something magical about Las Vegas for lovers, because a blushing couple ties the knot here every five minutes. Scores of celebrity couples have exchanged vows in Sin City, from Elvis Presley and Priscilla Beaulieu, to Sammy Davis Jr and Swedish model May Britt, to Andre Agassi and Steffi Graf. Why not you, too? After all, the 50-50 odds of a marriage surviving 'till death us do part' start to look pretty good in comparison to the chances of hitting a royal flush at the poker table. (You don't have to be sober to get married here either – that helps some folks a lot.)

Choices for the perfect spot to say 'I do' are endless. Weddings are performed in gondolas (p84) at the Venetian or atop the Eiffel Tower (p82) at Paris Las Vegas. You can hire an Elvis impersonator to serenade you with 'Blue Hawaii,' or dress up like Marilyn Monroe. You can even get married after a dramatic helicopter landing on the floor of the Grand Canyon (p85).

To be truthful, the more Vegas wedding chapels (p84) you see, the less you may be inclined to entrust them with the happiest day of your lives. Many are pretty tacky, full of plastic flowers, fake stained-glass windows and doll's-house pews. You'll feel rushed, as these places crank out dozens of weddings every day. Expect to pay upwards of $200 for a basic service, including a chintzy limo ride to the chapel.

Before you get hitched at a wedding chapel, stop by Clark County's **Marriage Bureau** (☎ 671-0600; www.accessclarkcounty.com/depts/clerk/Pages/marriage _information.aspx; 201 Clark Ave; ⏰ 8am-midnight) for a license ($55, cash only).

Overseas visitors should check back home first if they'll need any additional documentation to 'make it official.'

Valentine's Day and New Year's Day are crush times for Vegas wedding chapels; if you want to say your vows at peak times, apply for a license up to a year in advance online. Make wedding-chapel reservations as far in advance as possible, too. Otherwise, civil courthouse ceremonies are performed 8am to 10pm daily.

You don't have to elope to find romance in Sin City. Steal a kiss over mega martinis atop the Stratosphere Tower (p137), clasp hands as you watch the Bellagio's dancing fountains show (p80) or hide out with your paramour in a luxe suite all weekend (p26). Room service menus feature champagne, gourmet chocolate and XXX-goodies to spice up your love life.

If you're looking to explore your wilder side, Sin City infamously offers fantasy strip clubs (p152) and erotica shops (p90), all just a short cab ride away from the Strip. Or catch eye-popping burlesque acts over at jewel-like Forty Deuce (p153) cabaret inside Mandalay Bay.

BEST SECRET SMOOCHING SPOTS
> Downtown Cocktail Room (p134)
> Fireside Lounge (p134)
> Mix (p136)
> Red Rock Canyon (p160)
> West Wind Las Vegas Drive-In (p138)

MOST ROMANTIC RESTAURANTS
> Alizé (p125)
> Joël Robuchon (p108)
> Restaurant Guy Savoy (p104)
> Social House (p116)
> Vintner Grill (p129)

Top left Get cozy at Fireside Lounge (p134) **Above** Be romanced in the plush, intimate surrounds of Joël Robuchon (p108)

SNAPSHOTS

ARTS SCENE

If art imitates life, then Las Vegas must be a masterpiece, because it strives to imitate everywhere else on earth. It has a miniature Eiffel Tower, mock-medieval castles and Greek statuary copied from the masters. World-class exhibitions hit the Bellagio Gallery of Fine Art (p74), and the Las Vegas Art Museum (p76). Galleries (p74) in the 18b Arts District are where you'll find original works by local artists, especially on First Friday nights (p14).

Don't forget about Las Vegas' most famous art form: there are over 15,000 miles of neon tubing used for signage throughout the city. Start your DIY night-time neon art tour at the 'Welcome to Fabulous Las Vegas' sign (p81), then cruise the casinos of the Strip and downtown's Glitter Gulch, detouring to the Neon Museum (p76).

When it comes to live music (p139), casinos still book legendary entertainers just like in the 1950s and early '60s, when Frank Sinatra and his Rat Pack packed the house full. A few breakthrough local alt-rock bands have catapulted onto the national scene recently, such as the Killers and Panic! At the Disco. Vegoose (p132), an indie music-and-arts festival, comes with costumed partying over the Halloween weekend.

Hollywood fawns over Las Vegas, too, which is no surprise given that it's less than 300 miles from Los Angeles. CineVegas (p132) is a rising star on the indie film-festival circuit. For more on movies made here, see p186.

BEST ART GALLERIES
> Bellagio Gallery of Fine Art (p74)
> Commerce Street Studios (p76)
> Contemporary Arts Collective (Arts Factory; p74)
> Las Vegas Art Museum (p76)
> Neon Museum (p76)

COOLEST CASINO MIMETIC ARCHITECTURE
> Caesars Palace (p43)
> Luxor (p49)
> New York–New York (p53)
> Paris Las Vegas (p56)
> Venetian (p62; pictured above)

BUFFETS

Veterans of Vegas' 'groaning boards' proffer some sage words of advice. First, starve yourself for as long as possible before saddling up at a buffet, and don't count on eating any meals afterward. You'll get more for your money at breakfast or lunch – or better yet, weekend brunch – than at dinner, unless special entrées like steak or seafood are added.

Generally speaking, the more expensive the casino hotel, the better the fare. Famous buffets at Wynn Las Vegas (p117), Bellagio (p102), Planet Hollywood (p114), Paris Las Vegas (p113) and the Rio (p125) compete for the top honors in town. On Sundays, the House of Blues' (p140) gospel brunch is a stand-out; buy tickets in advance.

Once you wait out the queue at most buffets, the time-tested strategy is to grab teensy servings of everything before deciding what you really want to gorge on. Why get stuck with soggy sushi when a snappy chef is making fresh crepes or carving succulent roasted meats just a few food stations over? Always save room for multiple mini-desserts, from floating islands of caramel meringue to house-made gelato.

Oh, and don't forget to leave behind at least a dollar per person for the servers who bussed all those gluttonous piles of scrap-ridden plates off your table. It's only fair.

Fill your plate with global delicacies at Spice Market Buffet (p114)

GAY & LESBIAN LAS VEGAS

Nicknamed the Fruit Loop, the epicenter of Sin City's queer nightlife is about a mile east of the Strip, along Paradise Rd south of Harmon Ave and the Hard Rock casino hotel. Most bars, clubs and drag showrooms found here are oriented toward men, but host women-only nights. A more stealth gay scene orbits the Commercial Center, east of the Strip on Sahara Ave. Gay megaclub Kräve (p143) is the Strip's only predominantly queer venue.

Annual events include **Las Vegas Pride** (www.lasvegaspride.org) in May, and September's **BigHorn Rodeo** (www.bighornrodeo.com). To plug into the city's current scene, **QVegas** (www.qvegas.com) offers online downloads of the monthly magazine, which is also freely available at **Get Booked** (☎ 737-7780; www.getbooked.com; 4640 S Paradise Rd; ⏰ 10am-midnight Sun-Thu, 10am-2am Fri & Sat). Community websites include www.outinlasvegas.com and www.gaylasvegas.com. For social outings with local lesbians, join **Betty's Outrageous Adventures** (www.bettysout.com).

Although Vegas has a reputation as a wild party spot, most of its residents vote conservative. Same-sex public displays of affection aren't common or much appreciated by the moral majority in this conservative town. Civil unions and same-sex marriages aren't recognized by the state of Nevada, either.

BEST BETS FOR LGBT NIGHTLIFE
> FreeZone (p134; pictured above)
> Gipsy (p142)
> Goodtimes (p135)
> Kräve (p143)
> Piranha (p143)

BEST QUEER-FRIENDLY ATTRACTIONS & SHOWS
> Any Cirque du Soleil show (p144)
> Bette Midler (p145)
> *Jubilee!* Backstage Tour (p146)
> La Cage (p146)
> Liberace Museum (p79)

GREEN LAS VEGAS (SERIOUSLY)

Las Vegas (the meadows) lies at the edge of the vast Mojave Desert. In the parched rain shadow of the Sierra Nevada mountains, this flat city inhabits a bowl-shaped valley surrounded by mountain ranges. The population of the city already numbers over half a million, and if you count outlying suburbs and independent cities, the total number of people in the metro area is fast approaching two million, more than double what it was just a decade ago. Astoundingly, visitors outnumber locals nearly 20:1.

Because Las Vegas is an artificial playground built in the middle of the desert, is it any surprise that the valley may drain its entire water supply by the year 2021? Air pollution is another serious problem. The sky above the Strip is sometimes so dirty that you can't see the mountains for the haze. (For more on the city's environmental issues, see p184.)

But there's hope. An environmentally conscious educational complex, the Springs Preserve (p24 and p76) is literally a breath of fresh air. While other green spaces inside the city limits are rare, a few casino hotels have gardens (p77) for making your escape from the smoke-filled gaming areas. Along the Strip, ride the monorail (p190), a zero-emissions public transportation option. For excursions out of town, the Grand Canyon (p156), Red Rock Canyon (p160), Lake Mead and the Valley of Fire (p158) will satisfy your nature-loving soul.

The Springs Preserve is a major ecological achievement (p24 and p76)

LAS VEGAS WITH KIDS

Las Vegas half-heartedly sells itself as a family vacation destination. Because the legal gambling age is 21, many casino hotels and resorts would rather you simply left the little ones at home. Some high-end casino hotels even prohibit strollers from being on their grounds. State law prevents all minors from being in the gaming areas at all times.

Now, here's the good news. Las Vegas is full of family-friendly attractions and activities. Most casinos have virtual-reality and video game arcades, where even adults can have fun, such as the ESPN Zone Sports Arena (p82) at New York–New York, where a roller coaster shoots out of the Coney Island Emporium (p82), or Circus Circus' Adventuredome (p81). Teens will get a thrill atop the Stratosphere Tower (p84) and at Pole Position Raceway (p83). Some of the Strip's stage shows (including magic acts) welcome all-ages audiences. Speaking of which, kids can learn to do their own tricks at Houdini's Magic Shop (p98). For a fun, multimedia educational experience, make time to head out to the Springs Preserve (p24). Mandalay Bay's Shark Reef aquarium (p78; pictured below) and the MGM Grand's lion habitat (p77) are entertaining, as is the old-fashioned West Wind Las Vegas Drive-In (p138). Out-of-town excursions, especially to the Grand Canyon (p156), make for unforgettable family adventures. Surf to www.kidsinvegas.com for more city-specific advice and information.

BEST KID-FRIENDLY STAGE SHOWS
> Kà (p146)
> LOVE (p147)
> Mac King (p139)
> Mystère (p147)
> Phantom (p147)

FAST FAMILY-FRIENDLY EATS
> Cypress Street Marketplace (p103)
> Luv-It Frozen Custard (p120)
> Metro Pizza (p122)
> Stripburger (p105)
> Village Eateries (p110)

TEXAS HOLD'EM

A decade ago, Las Vegas visitors had a hard time finding a poker game. Many casinos, armed with profitability studies developed by MBAs, were replacing their card tables with high-limit slot machines. Ten years later, it's still hard to get a game in Vegas, but for an entirely different reason: poker has become the hottest game in town.

If you're one of those people who grew up playing wild draw poker games where the deuces, treys, one-eyed jacks, suicide kings and the queen who's not looking at the flower are all wild, you're in for a bit of a shock. While it's not the only game in town, Texas Hold'em is the most common. It's a fairly easy game to learn, but remarkably difficult to play well. Psychology helps.

The rules are simple. Each player is dealt two cards face down, known as hole cards. After a round of betting, three more cards – the 'flop' – are dealt face-up in the center of the table. These cards are community cards, shared by all the players still in the hand. After another round of betting, a fourth community card – the 'turn' – is dealt. After another round of betting, the fifth and final community card – the much-anticipated 'river' – is laid on the table. One last round of betting ensues, and the remaining players turn over their hole cards. The player who makes the strongest five-card hand (by combining his or her hole cards with three out of the five community cards) takes the pot.

TOP-RATED POKER ROOMS

> Bellagio (p40)
> Binion's (p42)
> Golden Nugget (p47)
> Venetian (p62)
> Wynn Las Vegas (p63)

BEST POKER READS

> *All In: The (Almost) Entirely True Story of the World Series of Poker* (Jonathan Grotenstein, 2005)
> *Hold 'em Poker for Advanced Players* (David Sklansky & Mason Malmuth, 1999)
> *Outplaying the Boys: Poker Tips for Competitive Women* (Cat Hulbert, 2005)
> *Poker: The Real Deal* (Phil Gordon & Jonathan Grotenstein, 2004)
> *Winning Low-Limit Hold'Em* (Lee Jones, 2005)

VINTAGE VEGAS

When it comes to Old Vegas, the slogan is 'Here today, gone tomorrow.' In a city that moves as fast as this one, priceless pieces of history get lost, bulldozed, imploded and discarded every day. So, if you want to devote a little time to unraveling the past in the present, hurry up and come see it while you still can.

Nothing says vintage Vegas more than the iconic 'Welcome to Fabulous Las Vegas' sign (see the boxed text, p81) south of the Strip. Except for maybe the Strip's original 1940s-era glam casino hotel, the Flamingo (p46), aka the folly that Bugsy built. Be sure to check out the yesteryear photos of movie stars and mobsters hidden by the valet-parking stand. At Bally's, you can catch a *Jubilee!* show (p145) after taking a behind-the-scenes tour led by a real showgirl or chorus boy (p146). East of the Strip at the Liberace Museum (p79), you can revel in more outlandish retro costumes.

If it's Elvis impersonators you're dying to see, search out the 'dealer-tainers' at the Imperial Palace (p78). Or you might catch sight of the King strolling along Las Vegas Blvd, past vintage casinos like the Sahara (p59) and wedding chapels (p84) galore, or in downtown's Fremont St, the heart of historic Glitter Gulch. There the Golden Gate casino hotel (p65) has been encouraging vice since 1906. Classier carpet joints like the Golden Nugget (p47) also have the sweet stench of Fabulous '50s glamour. You can play some good ol' no-limit poker with old-school cowboys in the back room at landmark Binion's (p42). Fremont St is a great place to search out spectacularly restored historical neon signs, too, courtesy of the Neon Museum (p76).

Get swept up in the nostalgia of the Sahara (p59)

The dramatic entrance of the Luxor (p49)

BACKGROUND
HISTORY

'What history?' you ask. Unlike the rest of the ruin-laden US Southwest, traces of Las Vegas' early history are scarce. The Uto-Aztecan-speaking Southern Paiute tribe of Native Americans inhabited the Las Vegas Valley for over a millennium before the Spanish Trail was blazed through this last area of the country to be explored by Europeans.

Contrary to Hollywood legend, there was much more at this crossroads in the Mojave Desert than a few ramshackle gambling houses, tumble-weeds and cacti the day that mobster Benjamin 'Bugsy' Siegel opened the tropical-themed Flamingo casino hotel under the searing desert sun.

TAMING THE FRONTIER

In 1829 Rafael Rivera, a scout for a Mexican trading expedition, was likely the first outsider to locate the natural springs in the Las Vegas Valley. Another traveler along the Spanish Trail, US Army officer John C Fremont arrived in 1844 to explore and map the area. Amid the hard-scrabble legions of miners who arrived later in the mid-19th century was a group of men hell-bent on doing God's work in Indian country. These Mormons were sent from Salt Lake City by leader Brigham Young to colonize the state of Deseret, their spiritual homeland. Their fort stood here for only two years. After the Civil War, small farms and ranches flourished in the valley.

In 1905 the driving of a golden spike in southern Nevada signaled the completion of a railroad linking Salt Lake City to Los Angeles (LA). Over two days, pioneers and real-estate speculators from LA bid for land, and lots in the Las Vegas townsite sold for up to 10 times their original price.

WEBSITES FOR PEEKING INTO THE PAST

> Classic Las Vegas (www.classiclasvegas.com)
> The First 100 (www.1st100.com)
> Las Vegas: An Unconventional History (www.pbs.org/wgbh/amex/lasvegas)
> Las Vegas Sun: History (www.lasvegassun.com/history)
> UNLV Special Collections (www.library.unlv.edu/speccol)

Top Left For a taste of the past, visit the Old Las Vegas Mormon Fort State Historic Park, north of the Strip **Bottom Left** Take a history lesson at Springs Preserve (p24 and p76)

BEST TOWN BY A DAM SITE

As the dust settled, the city of Las Vegas was officially founded. Sin quickly took root in a downtown red-light district known as Block 16. Home to gambling, booze and prostitution, this row of saloons, with their makeshift 'cribs' (brothels) out back, survived Nevada's several bans on gambling and the supposedly 'dry' years of Prohibition.

The federally sponsored Boulder (later Hoover) Dam project and the legalization of gambling carried Las Vegas through the Great Depression that followed the stock-market crash of 1929. Lax divorce requirements, quickie weddings, legalized prostitution and championship boxing bouts proved money-making bets for local boosters. New Deal dollars kept flowing into Southern Nevada's coffers right through WWII, which brought a huge air-force base to town, plus a paved highway to LA.

THE FABULOUS FIFTIES

Along with the rest of America, post-WWII Las Vegas felt like a boomtown again. Backed by East Coast mob money, gangster Benjamin 'Bugsy' Siegel opened the $6-million Flamingo casino hotel in 1946. With its incandescent pastel paint job, tuxedoed janitors, Hollywood entertainers and flashing neon, it became the model for the new Las Vegas to come.

Soon after, the Cold War justified constructing the Nevada Test Site. Initially unconcerned about radiation fallout, Las Vegans took the atomic age in stride. Monthly above-ground atomic blasts shattered casino windows downtown and mushroom clouds rose on the horizon, while the newly minted 'Atomic City' crowned a 'Miss Atomic Bomb' beauty queen, sold 'atomburgers' and billed Elvis as the 'Atomic-Powered Singer'.

NEVADA'S NUCLEAR DESERT

The US government stopped exploding nuclear bombs underground at the Nevada Test Site in 1992, but a nuclear future still looms large for state residents. US Department of Energy reports have been pushing for Yucca Mountain, only 100 miles northwest of Las Vegas, as the best location for the nation's only long-term radioactive nuclear-waste repository.

Did we say long-term? The proposed site, which would eventually hold 135,000 tons of spent nuclear fuel, would remain deadly for a million years. In that time, the earth itself may experience an ice age, and Yucca Mountain may no longer be one of the driest and most remote places in the lower 48 states.

FROM MOBSTERS TO MEGARESORTS

Big-name entertainers like Frank Sinatra, Liberace and Sammy Davis Jr arrived on stage at the same time as topless French showgirls, while mob-backed tycoons upped the casino-glitz ante. In the face of mounting bad publicity from notorious links to organized crime, the gambling industry was given a much-needed patina of legitimacy when eccentric billionaire Howard Hughes made the high-profile purchase of the Desert Inn in 1967.

Spearheaded by Hughes' spending spree, corporate ownership of casinos blossomed and publicly traded companies bankrolled a building bonanza in the late 1960s and early '70s. The 1973 debut of the original MGM Grand, now the world's largest hotel, and the launch of Steve Wynn's fabulous Mirage casino hotel in 1989 signaled that the age of the corporate 'megaresort' had dawned.

A MODERN MECCA

The 1990s saw the building boom on the Strip get even bigger, as the Luxor's gigantic black pyramid arose from the desert, the Stratosphere Tower became the tallest building in the western US, Paris Las Vegas erected its ersatz Eiffel Tower and the fountains of Bellagio started dancing.

The 21st century started off with an even bigger bang, as Steve Wynn imploded the vintage Desert Inn, then spent five years crafting his epony-mous megaresort. Today Las Vegas boasts all but a few of the world's 20 biggest hotels and nearly 40 million visitors every year. As slot machines go cashless and omnipotent surveillance goes digital, the illusions of Sin City approach an Orwellian dream-nightmare.

HERE TODAY, GONE TOMORROW

Structures that predate 1960 cling to Las Vegas like a trailer park hanging on for dear life during a tornado. Historic buildings are regularly blown to pieces with dynamite or slammed apart by wrecking balls, all to make way for new casino hotels and megaresorts.

Much like mushroom cloud–viewing parties during Nevada's atomic age, modern-day implosions are an excuse to party on the Strip. Out with a bang, not a whimper, is the motto. Tourists can buy videos of famous implosions from years past and learn all about the tricky technical matters requiring hundreds of pounds of explosives.

Everyone is eager to know what's next on the chopping block. There's even a web-site devoted entirely to Las Vegas casino 'death watches': www.jetcafe.org/npc/gambling/casino_death_watch.html.

LIFE IN LAS VEGAS

Known as America's dirty little secret, Sin City is a bastion of naughty, hangover-inducing weekends for people from all walks of life. Nevada's biggest metropolis sells itself to tourists with the slogan 'What happens here, stays here.' Infamous for its historic mob ties, Sin City's bad reputation obscures its day-to-day realities.

All of that belies what is, at heart, a conservative cow town. Despite all images to the contrary, prostitution is illegal in Clark County. Gay and lesbian life is often hidden, remaining underground to avoid the wrath of the religious right. Racism has a long history in Las Vegas, too; it wasn't until the 1960s that the color line was crossed at the Strip's casino hotels.

Las Vegas is a youthful city. Most locals were born outside the state. Many are twenty- and thirtysomethings who only moved here within the last five years (including a surprising number of people from Hawaii). Over 5000 people move to Las Vegas every month; what's less often reported is that another few thousand throw in the towel each month and leave. With so many new faces coming and going all the time, a disturbingly transient feeling permeates the city.

Lady Luck does not smile on everyone here. Las Vegas has been ranked as the 'meanest city in America' in which to be homeless. If you wander east of Fremont St or into the so-called 'Naked City' between downtown and the Strip, it won't take five minutes before you'll run into someone desperately in need of help: a crack-addicted prostitute looking to score, a babbling person pushing a shopping cart full of garbage bags or a degenerate gambler who's drunk off a 40oz beer can stuffed in a crumpled paper bag.

Nevada has the second-highest percentage of high-school dropouts in the country; since the local economy is fueled by minimum-wage workers, many teens think higher education won't help them get ahead. Fine arts and culture in Las Vegas would, until recently, have been just another oxymoron. That's no longer the case, however, with a thriving downtown arts scene, a couple of Smithsonian-affiliated museums and UNLV's Performing Arts Center.

Las Vegas is a city of die-hard sports fans, and there are scores of race and sports books inside casinos to prove it. The problem is, there aren't any professional home teams to root for. Most of the betting action is placed on national franchise teams, although UNLV college sports are big business. Everyone gets revved up for championship boxing matches on 'Fight Night.'

DOS & DON'TS

Polite requests will solve any problems you may have in Las Vegas faster than noisy complaints. For tipping practices, see p194.

The legal age for drinking and gambling is 21. You can buy booze everywhere 24/7.

No matter how old you are, always carry ID, especially for getting into bars and nightclubs. Open containers of alcohol are illegal in public but often overlooked, except in vehicles. Cops crack down on DUI (driving under the influence, whether of alcohol or drugs) with a vengeance; fines and sentences are stiff. On the street, more people are injured in crosswalks than in auto accidents.

Smoking cancer sticks is no longer permissible everywhere; stogie puffing is also restricted. A limited ban on smoking inside shopping malls, movie theaters, restaurants and some bars went into effect in 2006, but it's not universally observed or enforced. Hotels advertise nonsmoking guest rooms, but there are no guarantees – you may sniff more than a whiff of cigarettes inside 'em.

When movie stars first landed in Las Vegas in the 1950s, no lady would be caught dead in anything less than an evening gown once the cocktail hour arrived, and even off-duty showgirls dressed like starlets. Meanwhile, Sy Devore tailored European-style suits for the Rat Pack and even the janitors wore tuxedos at the Flamingo casino hotel. Today, dress codes exist only at high-end restaurants, trendy nightclubs and ultra lounges. T-shirts and jeans are the everyday norm.

GIRLS! GIRLS! GIRLS!

Prostitution was banned from Las Vegas in the 1940s, when the US military forced the closure of the city's brothels. But Mayor Oscar Goodman has gone on record with his pro-prostitution stance, saying that legalizing prostitution here would 'turn old motels into beautiful brothels.'

And then there's George Flint, an ordained minister who is Nevada's only paid lobbyist for the state's legal bordellos. His job is to see that attempts to end legal prostitution in Nevada, where it's still permitted in many rural counties, don't get too far.

Far from romantic Old West bordellos, most modern brothels are just double-wide trailers behind a barbed-wire fence at the side of a lonesome highway. For a real-life peek behind the scenes, read Alexa Albert's conflicted and disturbing *Brothel: Mustang Ranch and Its Women*, or catch an episode of HBO's ridiculous *Cathouse*.

GOVERNMENT & POLITICS

In 1999, in a major blow to official public-relations efforts to clean up Sin City's image, Las Vegas voters elected long-time criminal defense lawyer Oscar Goodman to be their mayor. Goodman, who gained fame as a notorious legal shark defending mobster 'goodfellas' like Tony 'The Ant' Spilotro and Meyer Lansky, even portrayed himself in the movie *Casino*. What's less well-known is that Goodman also devoted much of his practice to the poor and the dispossessed, sometimes working pro bono.

The alleged 'barrister to butchers,' as an editorial in the *Las Vegas Review-Journal* described him, makes no effort to hide his past. Indeed, Mayor Goodman loves to talk about the old days. But he caught the voters' fancy with a populist platform calling for developers to pay fees to help solve the city's traffic and pollution woes. The mayor has also been a tireless proponent of the need to redevelop the downtown urban core.

After being re-elected to a third mayoral term with a landslide 83.69% of the vote in 2007, Goodman is still enjoying enormous popularity. He frequently uses the mayoral pulpit for fiery comments on hot-button political issues, such as legalizing prostitution. His more notorious achievements include getting his mug on a limited-edition casino chip, becoming a guest celebrity photographer for *Playboy*, endorsing a brand of gin for $100,000 and hosting 'Martini with the Mayor' nights. Viva Las Vegas!

ENVIRONMENT

Las Vegas is an environmentalist's nightmare, the antithesis of a naturalist's vision of America. Ironically, it's also the gateway to some of the Southwest's most spectacular natural attractions, such as the Grand Canyon.

Water usage is the chief concern. The city of Las Vegas receives the vast majority of its water from the Colorado River, which feeds Lake Mead. Projections suggest that the Las Vegas Valley has a 50/50 chance of exhausting its entire water supply by 2021.

Air pollution is an equally vexing topic: the valley is fringed by mountains that trap hazardous particles, and the city is often in violation of federal air-quality standards. On many days the sky harbors a dirty inversion layer, sometimes so thick that the mountains are invisible. With traffic on the freeways and at McCarran International Airport on the rise, it's looking a lot like LA.

For more on 'greening' Las Vegas, see p173.

GREEN TOURISM TIPS
> Ride the zero-emissions monorail (p190)
> Take the Megabus (p188) instead of flying to Las Vegas
> Don't rent a car, unless you're taking a trip out of town (p155)
> Bring your own toiletries and reuse towels at your hotel; prevent unnecessary house-keeping by hanging the 'Do Not Disturb' sign on your door
> Stop buying plastic water bottles; instead, refill 'em with the city's perfectly drinkable tap water
> Recycle aluminum cans and plastic bottles at the Springs Preserve (p24 and p76)

FURTHER READING

Few famous authors have hit the jackpot in Vegas, but gonzo journalist Hunter S Thompson *(Fear and Loathing in Las Vegas: A Savage Journey to the Heart of the American Dream)*, 1960s countercultural narrator Tom Wolfe *(The Kandy-Kolored Tangerine-Flake Streamline Baby)*, and pop novelist and screenwriter Mario Puzo *(Inside Las Vegas)* have all confronted the underbelly of the shimmering beast.

Scores of pulpy biographies have been written about the gangsters, movie stars and entertainers who pushed this dusty Nevada town into the spotlight, from gangster Bugsy Siegel to Elvis and beyond. *Rat Pack Confidential: Frank, Dean, Sammy, Peter, Joey and the Last Great Show Biz Party* by Shawn Levy has a swingin' style that echoes the hip stylings of the era. *Cult Vegas: The Weirdest! The Wildest! The Swingin'est Town on Earth* by Mike Weatherford, an entertainment reporter for the *Las Vegas Review-Journal*, revels in all of the offbeat trivia and celebrity gossip from the 1960s 'golden age.' *When the Mob Ran Vegas: Stories of Murder, Mayhem and Money* dishes fantastic dirt on Sin City's gangster era, all told by Mafia aficionado Steve Fischer.

Nicholas Pileggi's *Casino: Love and Honor in Las Vegas* tracks the true-crime story of the Chicago mafia's move to take over Vegas, with all the bribery, book-making and mistresses leading in a downward spiral to disaster.

Equally dark in its outlook, John O'Brien's *Leaving Las Vegas* is a merci-less novel about a desperate alcoholic and an equally damaged 'working girl.' In *Skin City: Behind the Scenes of the Las Vegas Sex Industry*, long-time resident Jack Sheehan interviews madams, strippers and XXX-film stars for what a reviewer called an 'erotic travelogue.'

VINTAGE VEGAS SOUNDTRACK

> 'Luck Be a Lady,' as recorded by Frank Sinatra
> 'Viva Las Vegas,' as recorded by Elvis Presley
> 'Ace in the Hole,' as recorded by Bobby Darin
> 'The Lady is a Tramp,' as recorded by Sammy Davis Jr
> 'I've Got You Under My Skin,' as recorded by Keely Smith and Louis Prima

...or just about anything from Capitol Records' *The Rat Pack: Live at the Sands* album or the *Live from Las Vegas* series. For a red-light burlesque groove, the rare *Las Vegas Grind* series from Crypt Records (www.cryptrecords.com) should satisfy all of your naughty urges.

Titled as an homage to Upton Sinclair's muckraking novel *The Jungle*, Ed Reid and Ovid Demaris' *Green Felt Jungle* was an early indictment of casino corruption and lawless violence in Las Vegas during the 1940s, '50s and early '60s. Think all of the mobsters have left town and Vegas has been Disneyfied? Think again. *The Money and the Power: The Making of Las Vegas and Its Hold on America* by Sally Denton and Roger Morris is a haunting investigation of the city's underworld today.

For high-culture vultures, the landmark 1995 anthology *Literary Las Vegas*, edited by Mike Tronnes, features essays and short stories spanning 40 years, from atomic bomb–viewing picnics to the wedding-chapel industry. Robert Venturi's classic *Learning from Las Vegas* was the first to celebrate the city's architecture as pop art, and *Viva Las Vegas: After-Hours Architecture* by Alan Hess is an illustrated history of pre-Luxor properties.

FILMS & TELEVISION

Less than 300 miles from Los Angeles, Las Vegas has long been a favorite shooting location for Hollywood. Maybe it's the sheer cinematic quality of the Strip, which resembles a giant movie set, that draws so many directors here.

Casino interiors were cast often by the industry in the 1940s, when Frank Sinatra made his silver-screen debut and movie mogul Howard Hughes frequently worked on location. Atomic testing captured the imagination of B-grade sci-fi directors in the 1950s. Sinatra's Rat Pack enjoyed frequent cameos, especially after their hijinks in the classic *Ocean's 11* (1960), and Elvis shook his thang in *Viva Las Vegas* (1964). James Bond glorified glitzy Vegas in *Diamonds are Forever* (1971), while the epic

Godfather (1972), written by self-described 'degenerate gambler' Mario Puzo, was the first flick to portray the Mafia in Las Vegas. Martin Scorsese delved deeper into mobster wars with *Casino* (1995).

In *Rain Man* (1988), Dustin Hoffman and Tom Cruise conspire to beat the house edge. In *Bugsy* (1991), Warren Beatty and Annette Benning bring to life the original Flamingo casino hotel. Obviously infatuated with Sin City, Nicholas Cage starred with Sarah Jessica Parker in *Honeymoon in Vegas* (1992) and Elizabeth Shue in the brutal *Leaving Las Vegas* (1995). The epitome of bad taste, Chevy Chase's *Vegas Vacation* (1997) nevertheless had a few redeeming cameos, including Wayne Newton and Siegfried and Roy on stage at the Mirage.

No movie rebirthed the contemporary cool of Vegas as much as *Swingers* (1996) did. The cinematic adaptation of Hunter S Thompson's classic *Fear and Loathing in Las Vegas* (1998), starring Johnny Depp and Benicio Del Toro, confirmed that sin was 'in' again. In a remake of the Sinatra classic *Ocean's Eleven* (2001), a star-studded cast including Brad Pitt, George Clooney and Julia Roberts plots to bilk a string of casinos. The independent flick *The Cooler* (2003), featuring William H Macy as a no-luck gambler and Alec Baldwin as a monstrous casino mogul, is all aces. Starring Kevin Spacey, *21* (2008) was inspired by the true story of card-counting MIT college students who swindled Vegas casinos.

The prime-time TV show *CSI: Crime Scene Investigation* sets fictionalized police forensic investigations against the backdrop of Vegas' neon lights. Reality TV has hit Las Vegas like an epidemic, starting with MTV's *Real World: Las Vegas*. More recently, pop illusionist and stunt performer Criss Angel's *Mindfreak* is a runaway cable hit.

DIRECTORY

TRANSPORTATION

ARRIVAL & DEPARTURE

AIR

Las Vegas is served by **McCarran International Airport** (LAS; ☎ 261-5211; www.mccarran.com; 5757 Wayne Newton Blvd), just a crapshoot from the south end of the Strip, and a few smaller general aviation facilities around the city. McCarran ranks among the USA's 10 busiest airports. Most domestic airlines use Terminal 1; international, charter and some domestic flights depart from Terminal 2. Free trams link outlying gates. There are ATMs, a full-service bank, post office, first-aid and police stations, the club **24 Hour Fitness** (day pass $10), and free wi-fi internet access. Left-luggage lockers are unavailable.

Taxi & Limousine

Taxis to Strip hotels (allow at least 30 minutes in heavy traffic) are $13 to $22 (cash only, plus tip); fares to downtown average $24. The queue at the airport can be excruciatingly long; arriving passengers can usually find a skycap (airport porter) in the baggage-claim area, tip $5 or $10 per cart, then skip to the front of the line. 'Long-hauling' through the airport connector tunnel to I-15 is common; tell your driver to use Paradise Rd or other direct surface routes. From the airport, it costs at least $45 per hour for a chartered sedan, or $57 for a six-person stretch limo.

CLIMATE CHANGE & TRAVELING TO LAS VEGAS

Travel – especially air travel – is a significant contributor to global climate change. At Lonely Planet, we believe that all travelers have a responsibility to limit their personal impact. As a result, we have teamed with Rough Guides and other concerned industry partners to support Climate Care, which allows travelers to offset the greenhouse gases they are responsible for with contributions to energy-saving projects and other climate-friendly initiatives in the developing world. Lonely Planet offsets all staff and author travel.

Flying is not the only way to reach Sin City, though. **Megabus** (☎ 877-462-6342; www.megabus.com) offers three daily express buses between downtown LA (Union Station) and Las Vegas, taking four to five hours each way. At press time, one-way fares ranged from $1 to $37. In Las Vegas, the Megabus station is near the UNLV campus, a short taxi or bus ride east of the Strip. A high-speed rail link between Southern California and Las Vegas along the heavily trafficked I-15 corridor has been proposed, but no dice yet.

For more information about responsible travel, visit www.lonelyplanet.com. For details on offsetting your carbon emissions and a carbon calculator, go to www.climatecare.org.

Bus

Notoriously slow airport-shuttle buses charge $6 per person to the Strip, and $7.50 to downtown or off-Strip hotels. Some airport shuttles operate 24 hours.

If you're traveling light, CAT's bus 108 runs between 5am and 2am from the airport to the convention center, Hilton and Sahara monorail stations ($1.25, 20 to 30 minutes), then continues downtown. Bus 109 runs 24/7 between the airport and the Downtown Transportation Center ($1.25, 30 to 60 minutes), a short walk from Fremont St.

LAND

By car it's about a 4½-hour drive (270 miles) from Los Angeles, five hours (330 miles) from San Diego and 9½ hours (570 miles) from San Francisco. Expect serious delays on weekends and holidays. For recorded road-condition updates, dial ☎ 877-687-6237 for Nevada and ☎ 800-427-7623 for California. Along the I-15 corridor through the Mojave Desert, Highway Radio (Barstow 98.1FM, Baker 99.5FM) broadcasts traffic and weather updates every half hour.

TRAVEL DOCUMENTS

Foreign visitors must have a machine-readable passport that has biometric identifiers and is valid for at least six months beyond their planned exit date.

VISA

Visas aren't required for citizens of the 27 Visa Waiver Program countries (including Australia, Ireland, New Zealand, the UK and many other European nations), who may enter the USA for up to 90 days visa-free. As of 2009, citizens of these countries need to register online with the government three days before their visit (see http://travel.state.gov/web); this registration is valid for two years. Temporary visitors from Canada do not normally need a visa, but must bring their passport. All other foreign citizens must wrangle a non-immigrant visa in advance from a US embassy or consulate. Double-check the mercurial requirements at http://travel.state.gov/visa.

RETURN/ONWARD TICKET

Travelers under the reciprocal visa-waiver program need round-trip or onward tickets to enter the US. Travelers applying for visas overseas will generally require such tickets as proof of their intent to skedaddle home.

GETTING AROUND

Las Vegas traffic is often grid-locked and the most heavily touristed areas are flat, so the best way to get around is on foot, in combination with occasional taxi, monorail or bus rides. In this book, the nearest monorail station (**M**) or bus route (🚌) is noted after the relevant icon with each listing.

BUS

Citizens Area Transit (CAT; ☎ 228-7433, 800-228-3911; www.catride.com) operates from 5:30am to 1am daily, with the most popular Strip and downtown routes running 24/7. The fare is $1.25 ($2 for double-decker Deuce buses along Las Vegas Blvd); exact change is required. Free maps and timetables are available from drivers and the **Downtown Transportation Center** (300 N Casino Center Blvd).

Some off-Strip casino hotels offer limited free shuttle buses to/from the Strip.

CAR

Heavy traffic makes navigating the city by car a chore, particularly during weekday rush hours and on weekends along the Strip. When traffic is snarled on I-15 and Las Vegas Blvd, stick to alternate surface routes. Listen to KNUU 'K-News' (970AM) for frequent traffic and weather updates. Free valet (tip at least $2) and/or self-parking are available almost everywhere in Las Vegas. If you've been drinking, **Designated Drivers** (☎ 702-456-7433; 🕐 24hr) will pick you up and drive your car back to your hotel; fees vary, depending on mileage.

At press time, gas cost under $4 per US gallon in Las Vegas. Econ-

omy car-rental rates start at around $25 per day or $135 per week, plus $10 to $15 per day for insurance (usually optional). Corvettes and exotic convertibles fetch over $200 per day. Expect to pay sales taxes of up to 7.5%, governmental-service fees of 10%, a customer facility charge ($3 per day) and 10% airport surcharge. For weekends, reserve at least two weeks in advance.

Car-rental agencies with airport desks include **Alamo** (☎ 800-462-5266; www.alamo.com), **Budget** (☎ 800-922-2899; www.budgetvegas.com), **Dollar** (☎ 800-800-3665; www.dollar.com) and **Thrifty** (☎ 800-847-4389; www.thrifty .com). Airport pick-ups are usually cheaper than having a rental car delivered to your hotel. For something glamorous, ring **Rent-A-Vette** (☎ 800-372-1981; www.rent-a-vette.com; 5021 Swenson St).

MONORAIL & TRAM

A private **monorail** (☎ 699-8299; www .lvmonorail.com; 🕐 7am-2am Mon-Thu, to 3am Fri-Sun) links some properties along the Strip's resort corridor, speedily shuttling between the MGM Grand, Bally's/Paris, the Flamingo, Harrah's, the convention center, the Hilton and the Sahara. One-way rides cost $5; multi-ride discounts are available.

Free air-conditioned trams shuttle between TI (Treasure Island) and the Mirage; and Excalibur, Luxor and Mandalay Bay.

TAXI

It's illegal to hail a cab on the street. Taxi stands are found at casino, hotel and shopping-mall entrances. Fares (cash only) are metered: flagfall is $3.30 plus $2.65 per mile and 50¢ while waiting. A lift from one end of the Strip to the other, or from mid-Strip to downtown, runs from $12 to $16, plus tip. Reputable companies include **Yellow/Checker/Star** (☎ 873-2000). File any complaints via http://taxi.state.nv.us.

TRAVEL PASSES

Monorail passes cost $15/40 for one/three days. CAT's 24-hour bus pass is $5.

PRACTICALITIES

BUSINESS HOURS

Open 24/7/365 is the rule at casino hotels. Normal business hours are 9am to 5pm on weekdays. Some banks and post offices stay open later and on Saturday mornings. Retail shopping hours are 10am to 9pm (to 6pm Sunday); casino shops stay open until 11pm or later. Christmas is one of the few holidays on which most non-casino businesses close.

DISCOUNTS

The biggest discounts are 'comps' handed out by casinos to members of slot clubs and 'rated'

gamblers. Casino 'fun books,' usually given only to guests but sometimes available to those who ask, are a grab bag of discount coupons. Hotel rooms provide complimentary copies of industry promo magazines, such as *What's On* and *Las Vegas Magazine + Showbiz Weekly,* that are the source of bigger discounts (eg half-price or two-for-one admission) on shows, restaurants and attractions.

A **Las Vegas Power Pass** (☎ 800-490-9330; www.visiticket.com; adult/child from $75/42.50) may be worthwhile if you plan to visit a *lot* of big-ticket attractions and museums; it even lets you skip the lines at some of them. Don't bother buying the MealTicket or ShoppersTicket.

ELECTRICITY

Electrical current in the USA is 110 volts AC (60Hz). North American electrical goods have plugs with two (flat) or three (two flat, one round) pins. Consult www.kropla.com for information about converters and adapters.

EMERGENCIES

On the Strip and the Fremont Street Experience, police and private security officers are out in force, and surveillance cameras (the 'eye in the sky') are omnipresent. Utilize in-room hotel safes and never leave valuables unattended, especially while gambling. Beware of pickpockets in crowds (eg on public transportation). If you wander away from Fremont St downtown, keep your wits about you, day and night.

For emergencies:
Police, fire, ambulance (☎ 911)
Police (non-emergency) (☎ 311)
Rape Crisis Center (☎ 366-1640)

For minor ailments and injuries, it's less expensive to go to a walk-in clinic than a hospital emergency room. East of the Strip, **Harmon Medical Center** (☎ 796-1116; 150 E Harmon Ave; ☾ 24hr) offers discounts for uninsured patients, limited translation services and courtesy transportation. Emergency contraception services are available without a prescription from **Planned Parenthood** (☎ 547-9888; Suite 54, 3320 E Flamingo Rd).

HOLIDAYS

New Year's Day January 1
Martin Luther King Jr Day Third Monday in January
Presidents' Day Third Monday in February
Easter Sunday March/April
Memorial Day Last Monday in May
Independence Day July 4
Labor Day First Monday in September
Columbus Day Second Monday in October
Veterans' Day November 11
Thanksgiving Day Fourth Thursday in November
Christmas Day December 25

INTERNET

Most hotels have business centers that charge an arm and a leg for 24/7 internet access. The most reliable free wi-fi hotspots are off-Strip at the convention center and airport. High-speed wired/wireless internet access in hotel rooms typically costs more than $10 per 24 hours. Cheap internet cafés hide inside Strip souvenir shops south of Harmon Ave, and across from the UNLV campus along Maryland Parkway. Otherwise, try **FedEx** (East of the Strip ☎ 951-2400; 395 Hughes Center Dr; per min 10-30¢; ☾ 24hr; downtown ☎ 383-7022; 830 S 4th St; per min 10-30¢; ☾ 7am-9pm Mon-Fri, 9am-5pm Sat).

For the lowdown on what's happening on the Strip and downtown, die-hard Vegas visitors and newbies alike can check out these sites:
Cheapo Vegas (www.cheapovegas.com)
Las Vegas Advisor (www.lasvegasadvisor.com)
Las Vegas Logue (www.lasvegaslogue.com)
LVCVA (www.visitlasvegas.com)
Raw Vegas (www.rawvegas.tv)
vegas.com (www.vegas.com)

MONEY

Casinos exist to separate you from your dough and will facilitate that end any way they can. Transaction fees at ATMs inside gaming areas are high ($3.50 or more). All casinos will advance cash against plastic, but fees are exorbitant – don't do it. To avoid surcharges, use your debit card to get cash back when making purchases at non-casino businesses like convenience stores and pharmacies.

For currency exchange rates, see the inside front cover of this book. Casino-hotel fees to exchange foreign currency are higher than at banks but lower than at most exchange bureaus. **American Express** (☎ 739-8474; Fashion Show, 3200 Las Vegas Blvd S; ☻ 10am-9pm Mon-Fri, 10am-8pm Sat, noon-6pm Sun) has competitive rates.

The average visitor's daily budget is $250. Accommodations will be your biggest expense, and hotel room rates go up and down like the stock market (see p164). Meals cost at least $10, though they can easily run over $100 per person. You don't need to rent a car, except for jaunts outside the city (see p155). For more tips on saving money at attractions and on dining and entertainment, see p191.

NEWSPAPERS & MAGAZINES

Nevada's largest daily newspaper is the conservative Las Vegas Review-Journal (www.lvrj.com), which publishes with the tabloid Las Vegas Sun (www.lasvegassun.com); look for the former's Friday 'Neon' entertainment guide. Free tabloids Las Vegas Weekly (www.lasvegas weekly.com), weekly Las Vegas CityLife (www.lasvegascitylife.com) and bimonthly Vurb (www.vurb magazine.com) cover local news, nightlife, music, film, the arts and more. Free monthly magazine 944 (www.944.com/lasvegas) tracks celebs, clubs and hot spots. Monthly Las Vegas Life (www.lvlife .com) has restaurant reviews and fine-arts listings. Vegas (www.vegas magazine.com) targets fashionistas, casino moguls and celebrities.

ORGANIZED TOURS

Gray Line (☎ 384-1234, 800-634-6579; www.graylinelasvegas.com) Runs the popular 'Neon Lights' night-time city bus tour, which lasts six hours ($45); stops include the Bellagio's fountains and downtown's Fremont Street Experience.

Haunted Vegas Tours (☎ 737-5540, reservations 866-218-4935; www.hauntedvegas tours.com; 2½hr show & tour $57; ☻ 9:30pm Sat-Thu) Most folks are disappointed by the campy sideshow, but the after-dark bus trip around Sin City visits the haunts of Liberace and gangster Bugsy Siegel.

Jubilee! Backstage Tour (☎ 946-4567; Bally's, 3645 Las Vegas Blvd S; 1hr tour $10-15; ☻ 11am Mon, Wed & Sat) Escorted by a real-life stage performer, Bally's takes you behind the scenes of Vegas' long-running $50-million showgirl revue, Jubilee!

Papillon Grand Canyon Helicopters (☎ 736-7243, 888-635-7272; www.papillon .com) Offers 10-minute jetcopter flyovers of the Strip (from $69).

Vegas Mob Tour (☎ 737-5540, reservations 866-218-4935; www.vegasmobtour.com; 2½hr film & tour $57; ☻ 7pm Sat-Thu) This night-time city bus tour revels in the sordid history of when the mafia really ran this town.

TELEPHONE

The USA uses a variety of cellular-phone systems, most of which are incompatible with the GSM 900/1800 standard used throughout Europe, Asia and Africa. Most North American visitors can use their cell phones in Las Vegas, but check with your carrier about roaming charges before you start racking up minutes. Using cell phones near casino race and sports books is prohibited by law. On the Strip, some hotel business centers rent out cell phones to guests.

Public phones are mostly coin-operated; some accept credit cards or have dataports for laptop and PDA internet access. Local calls generally cost 35¢. If calling a long-distance number outside the local area code (☎ 702), dial ☎ 1 first. Pharmacies and convenience stores sell prepaid phonecards, but they can be rip-offs – check the fine print for hidden fees and surcharges. Major carriers like **AT&T** (☎ 800-321-0288) can facilitate long-distance calls.

COUNTRY & CITY CODES
City code (☎ 702)
Country code (☎ 1)

USEFUL PHONE NUMBERS
Local Operator (☎ 0)
International Operator (☎ 00)
International Direct Dial Code (☎ 011)
Local Directory Assistance (☎ 411)

Long-distance Directory Assistance
(☎ 1 + area code + 555-1212)
Toll-free Directory Assistance
(☎ 800-555-1212)

TIPPING

Service-industry staff rely on tips to bring their incomes up to decent levels, while fortunes have been made by valet-parking concession owners. You should only withhold tips in cases of outrageously poor service, however. See the inside front cover of this guidebook for advice on who to tip, and how much.

TOURIST INFORMATION

Many tour operators push unofficial 'visitor information,' but there's only one official city tourism agency: **Las Vegas Convention & Visitors Authority** (LVCVA; ☎ 892-0711, 877-847-4858; www.visitlasvegas.com; 3150 Paradise Rd; ☒ office 8am-5pm, toll-free hotline 6am-9pm). The hotline provides up-to-date information about shows, attractions, activities and more, and staff may be able to help with finding last-minute accommodations.

TRAVELERS WITH DISABILITIES

Vegas has the most ADA-accessible guestrooms in the USA. Unless otherwise noted, all attractions listed in this book are wheelchair-accessible. Wheelchair seating is widely available and assisted listening devices are offered at most showrooms. Most public transportation and several hotel pools are lift-equipped. By law, all taxi companies must have a wheelchair-accessible van. If you're driving, bring your disabled-parking placard from home. Guide dogs may be brought into restaurants, hotels and businesses. Some payphones are equipped for the hearing-impaired. For more info, contact the LVCVA's ADA coordinator at ☎ 892-0711 (voice relay ☎ 800-326-6888, TTY ☎ 800-326-6868).

>INDEX

See also separate subindexes for Casinos (p200), See (p201), Shop (p201), Eat (p202) and Play (p203).

000 map pages

000 map pages

>MAPS

Revel in the nonstop carnival atmosphere of Las Vegas

589

Commercial
Center

Vegas Valley Dr

Las Vegas
Country
Club

Bel Air Dr

E Desert Inn Rd

Swenson St

Sierra Vista Dr

Twain Ave

Beverly Way

Sherwood St

Karen Ave

Joe W Brown Dr

Edison
Ave

Circle

St Louis Ave

E Sahara Ave

Las Vegas Hilton

Las Vegas
Convention
Center

Elm Dr

Cassella Dr

To Downtown
(1.5mi)

Paradise Rd

Sahara

605

S Paradise Rd

Mel Ave

Stratosphere

Boston Ave

Baltimore Ave

Cleveland Ave

Cincinnati Ave

Tam Dr

604

Sahara

Riviera Blvd

Riviera

Convention Center Dr

Country Club La

Western Ave

Circus Circus Dr

Circus Circus

Las Vegas Blvd S (The Strip)

THE
STRIP

Wynn
Las Vegas

Sands Ave

Sands Expo
Convention
Center

Desert Inn Rd Super-Arterial

Palazzo

Venetian

Casino Royale

TI (Treasure
Island)

Industrial Rd

Vegas Plaza Dr

Mirage

15

Kings Way

Westwood Dr

Highland Dr

W Sahara Ave

Alcoa Ave

Merritt Ave

Kings Ave

Richfield Blvd

Milo Way

Rigel Ave

Meade Ave

Sirius Ave

Alderbaran
Ave

Spring Mountain Rd

Polaris Ave

Procyon Ave

S Valley View Blvd

Sheridan
St

W Desert Inn Rd

Pioneer Ave

Renate Dr

Vanessa Dr

Schiff Dr

Twain Ave

589

El Conlon Ave

Tara Ave

Penwood Ave

Wing St

Wynn Rd

DOWNTOWN

9th St

To Cushman
Field (0.3mi)

E Bonanza Rd

604

Mesquite Ave

Stewart Ave

Fremont St

582

11th St

10th St

Carson Ave

9th St

8th St

Las Vegas Blvd N

El Cortez

7th St

5th St

Neonopolis

6th St

Clark Ave

Stewart Ave

Ogden Ave

Fitzgeralds

4th St

Las Vegas Blvd S

Downtown
Transportation
Center

Fremont St Experience

3rd St

Binion's

Main Street
Station

California

Golden Nugget

Bridger Ave

Lewis Ave

Vegas Club

95

Golden
Gate

93

Plaza

515

Main St

Casino Center Blvd

1st St

Bonneville Ave

Garces Ave

To Stratosphere
(1.5mi)

Mesquite Ave

Grand Central Pkwy

Gass St

Discovery Dr

15

400 m

0.2 miles

Las Vegas
Premium
Outlets

0

0